PICASSO

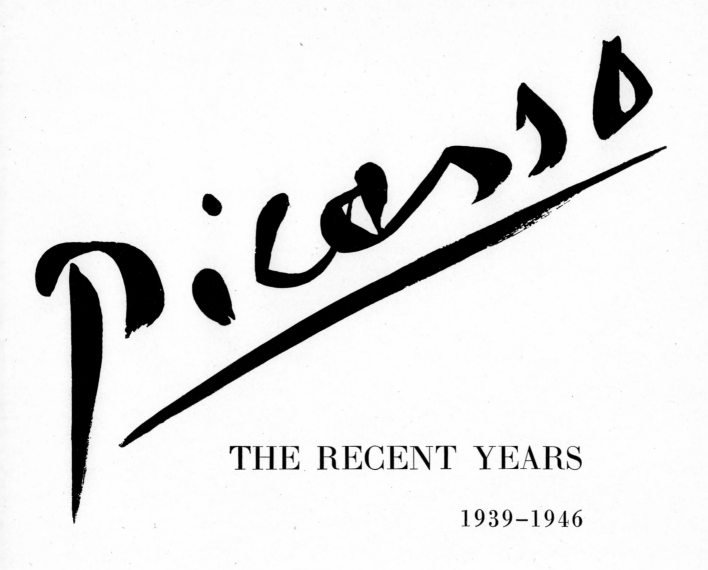

THE RECENT YEARS

1939–1946

HARRIET AND SIDNEY JANIS

DOUBLEDAY & COMPANY, INC.

GARDEN CITY, NEW YORK, 1946

PLATE 1

Picasso in his Studio at 7 Rue des Grandes Augustines, winter of 1944–5.
His Afghan hound, Kazbec, is now dead.

CLOSED in for five years by the dread silence of Gestapo censorship, Picasso emerged so great a figure after the war that almost universal interest was manifested in him. The wide inquiry that began immediately with the liberation of France revealed the fact that he had done an enormous amount of highly stimulating work, none of which, of course, had been exhibited anywhere during the war period. For this reason it seemed imperative to the authors, who had long planned a book on Picasso and his art, to set aside temporarily the original plan covering his life's work and to concentrate, instead, on the artist and his work during the war years. While the theme of these years furnishes the core of the book, work done since the close of the war and up to the present is included as indispensable to the consideration of the subject.

Up to the time of writing, though a number of exhibits have been held in postwar Europe, only one painting and a limited number of reproductions have been seen in America. In view of the lapse here of almost seven years, 1939 to 1946, the present publication of more than one hundred reproductions of this embattled phase may constitute the same challenge to the American art public as the exhibitions of the works themselves did in Europe. Responsible for this to a large degree is the fact that while the latest phase of Picasso has always been difficult to accept immediately, the paintings made during the war period strike the observer with perhaps the most overpowering impact of any he has ever done. Upon extended and closer study, however, his manner of expression in any period ceases to seem arbitrary as it takes its position within the framework of aesthetic and spiritual values which ultimately become apparent.

The text is divided into four chapters following which it continues in a running commentary that accompanies the pictures reproduced. Rather than give detailed and thorough analyses of a few paintings, the authors decided on brief descriptive comments that would cover a wide range of pictures, and the aggregate of these includes the many aspects, plastic, psychological, symbolic, humorous, witty, macabre, or fanciful which are to be encountered in the vast range of Picasso's creative work. Hitherto unpublished findings made throughout the text may be questioned; the work itself is invariably the source of these, and in each case analytical reference is made to the specific examples used for documentation. Regardless of the aspects discussed in the text, each picture reproduced has been selected primarily on the basis of aesthetic content.

The reproductions, so far as possible, are presented in sequences oriented to the points made in the text. They are, consequently, not necessarily in chronological order. A number of pertinent documentary photographs have been included as well, with a special attempt to show the original subject matter and the manner in which the artist has transformed it through the creative process.

Conclusions have been developed not only through study of the war period itself and its effect on Picasso, but, as well, through research into phases of the past in Picasso's work. In this way it was possible to view the work of the war years from a wider perspective and, in fact, only through this way can this period be sufficiently evaluated and its full significance comprehended. The relationship between the earlier cubist practices and those of recent years was found to be especially close, while it became more evident than ever that the different periods in Picasso's work are variations of his original, basic ideas and processes rather than the abrupt changes they are too frequently thought to be.

Besides the reference in the text to specific examples and photographs, documentation also consists of quotations from Picasso, many of them obtained in conversation with him during February and March 1946. Much additional material of historical and aesthetic interest derives from conversations during the same time with many of Picasso's closest friends.

The authors deeply appreciate the many kindnesses extended by Picasso himself, whose great generosity and warm encouragement made it possible to examine and study at firsthand, over a period of many weeks, the vast quantity of work in all media in his studio, and for his permission to have them photographed. Thanks are also due to Picasso's lifelong friend and secretary, M. Jaime Sabartés, for generously furnished and valuable information and for the weeks he patiently devoted while Picasso's works were being photographed in his studio and elsewhere. A debt of gratitude is owed to Picasso's many friends in Paris, London, and New York, who assisted enthusiastically in various ways; to Miss Dora Maar for her kind permission to reproduce a number of fine examples in her collection; to Mmes. Cuttoli, Louise Leiris and M. A. Behrendt, and Ms. Pierre Loeb, Louis Carré, D. H. Kahnweiler, Etienne Bignou, E. Teriade, S. Lapina, Henri Laugier, Yves Sjöberg, Julio Alvarez del Vayo, Michel de Brunoff, Gaston de Sainte-Croix, Donald Elder, A. Zwemmer, Martin B. Grossman, L'Association Française d'Action Artistique, and the British Council; and to the photographers Brassai, Chevojon, Hervochon, Vaux, Laneipce, Francis Lee, and George Holton; finally to Miss Sabra Mallett and Mr. Paul Hollister for their diligence in seeing the book through the arduous phases of production.

New York, July 1946.

CONTENTS

(Unless otherwise noted reproductions are of paintings in the collection of the artist)

LIST OF
PLATES

x i i

1 THE ARTIST AND THE WAR

THE FIGURE of Picasso has for almost half a century stood for more than artist; it has stood for the whole challenge which the concept *modern* throws, not merely to our complacency, but to the supposedly basic way of living and thinking to which we have adhered for centuries. With the advent of war, Picasso, with this almost universal quality of his nature, became all at once a symbol of the effect of war on the spiritual integrity, even life, of the individual human being. As the conflict swept over Europe, engulfing country after country and one cultural center after another, Picasso was discussed more than any other artist who had remained in Europe. Completely lost in the anonymity of war, his possible fate became a matter of general interest throughout the world.

During this time he was variously reported in the south of France, in Spain, in a German concentration camp, in the French Army, at the front. His studio was reported looted, his works destroyed. He was stigmatized by irresponsible persons as having turned reactionary in art, as living in luxury, as collaborating with the Nazis and selling his paintings to them. Immediately after the liberation, even on the very day of liberation, he was the one artist, above all others, sought out by G.I.'s, correspondents, and Allied friends. They found him in Paris, where he had been working almost obsessively, and living away from everyone except his closest friends, all of them tireless workers in the Underground. The fact that Picasso was safe in Paris and had been extremely productive was news of front-page importance. A flood of articles and newsspreads began to appear in the press of the world. Public interest in his whereabouts, welfare, and activities reached world-wide proportions. Many languages were needed to give the details of his survival to all those interested.

2

This interest is centered on a personality whose very name is a fetish of our time—one that for many years has had the power to evoke devoted partisanship or violent opposition. For Picasso has been a dynamic and controversial figure in art for almost fifty years and is today still the most creatively challenging artist working. Not only is he the focal point of the battle between the conservatives and the progressives, but many painters who have strongly admired his work have come so fully under the domination of its energy and force that they have rebelled against it as furiously as, though more transparently than, his bitterest enemies. After the liberation, the eyes of the world focused on him at once to see what had befallen him in the long war period.

Picasso, though sixty-three at the time of the liberation in 1944, and despite the hard years in occupied Paris, remained youthful and animated in spirit. His hair slightly grayer and the creases of his smile deepened by excessive leanness, his eye, nevertheless, still retained all its sharpness and sparkle. The spirit that had sustained him and had impelled him through these dark years to paint the most forceful and authoritative canvases of his career is in reality his own informing power, intensified by the will to resist the disruptive forces of war.

It was discovered that he had acted in the interim with characteristic principle, decisiveness, individuality, and humanity. At the outbreak of war Picasso had been in the south of France, in the town of Royan. Not long after the fall of Paris, when the only reasonable course open to leaders of culture was flight, he rushed defiantly back to Paris to remain there for the duration. Working prodigiously at painting and sculpture, refusing, despite privations, the Nazi comforts proffered by officers who, against party orders, hoped to buy his contraband art, he refused also to participate in any of the art programs in which other famous artists, either through coercion or through weak and misguided volition, were collaborating.

Nearly the whole civilized world knew the painting, *Guernica*, the epically historic protest against the brutal and wanton destruction in

1937,[1] of a Spanish town by Nazi experimental war equipment. That the creator of this historic painting, Picasso, had lived boldly in the very midst of the same Nazi ruthlessness, immediately fired the sympathy and imagination of the rest of the world, just as it had members of the Resistance Movement within France itself. Through his courage and integrity, Picasso emerged from the lost years of the war a personality of inspirational magnitude wholly commensurate with his stature as an artist.

The symbolic courage that had saved him during enemy occupation proved an irresistible magnet to all with the advent of liberation, and Picasso, who for many years had demanded quiet and time in which to work, now threw open his studio doors, especially to the American G.I.'s, thousands of whom clamored to visit him. Each week many hundreds made the pilgrimage, occasionally bringing as gifts the chewing gum, cigarettes, and chocolate bars obtainable only at canteens.

They found the painter living simply, working in his large top-floor studio—the room containing the famous many-tiered stove reproduced in Plate 1. This stove, like most of the stoves in Paris, had remained unlit during occupation years for want of fuel: Picasso had steadfastly refused the coal offered by the Nazis as a "gift borne by the Greeks." Even months after the liberation, when cordwood was obtainable, this stove, in itself a remarkable piece of industrial sculpture, served only as a flue to the smaller one seen in the foreground of the photograph. Because the temperature of the room was often below freezing, Picasso had difficulty painting at this time. Later, in the winter of 1945–46, when some fuel was obtainable, he did no painting at this studio, explaining: "It is impossible, because of the cold." In spite of the cold, he was doing some painting elsewhere, at an undisclosed address. He worked also at graphic art at the engraver's rather than in his own studio. Yet the complete lack of fuel during the war had proved a driving incentive.

In the years of their rule, the Gestapo had on several occasions vis-

[1]Three days later, on May 1, Picasso began work on *Guernica*.

ited Picasso's atelier. His imposing fame, coupled with the probable effect on French morale if he were molested, served to protect him. While the Nazis were stripping most of occupied Europe of its art treasures, they did not once attempt to loot his studio. This is especially surprising since his paintings might have served a number of purposes: as anti-modern art propaganda in Germany itself, for hostage value, or for sale abroad. Many of his paintings had been stored in a vault under a bank in Montparnasse; the rest, perhaps 200, were in his studio. Only one picture suffered damage during the war, a painting that was being reproduced in color at the engraver Lacourière in Montmartre (Plate 104). This picture was, ironically, damaged by friend rather than enemy, being hit by flying glass during one of the British Air Force night bombings of La Chapelle (Gare du Nord).

When Picasso opened his studio in liberated Paris to the G.I.'s and others, his first inquiries were concerning the artists in exile: Duchamp, Breton, Dali, Masson, and many others. He disclosed to his questioners that German officers repeatedly had tried to buy his pictures only to be categorically rejected. When, on the other hand, some German privates risked orders to visit him, he gave them a few small sketches, a gesture that in itself indicates the simple, basic democracy of his character. He explained how he had been able to work in the face of Nazi occupation and the party's antagonism to all forms of modern art, saying: "It was not a time for the creative man to fail, to shrink, to stop working," and "there was nothing else to do but work seriously and devotedly, struggle for food, see friends quietly, and look forward to freedom." In actuality, however, his activity carried considerably further than this explanation would imply. "Work," for example, included surreptitiously casting in forbidden, strategic metals the plasters he had made during the war as well as most of the earlier plaster sculpture of the thirties. This feat he had accomplished with the aid of Resistance friends, who made frequent nightly trips between his studio and the Underground foundry. The plasters and bronzes were transported under the very noses of the Nazis, cleverly concealed in wheelbarrows and carts ostensibly filled with rubbish—a nice diversion to constructive purposes of metals earmarked for destructive enemy use.

Picasso's productivity during the five war years yielded an amount equal to many an artist's lifework. It is estimated that he made at least 300, perhaps as many as 400 oils on canvas, five times that many sketches and drawings in ink, pencil, and oil on paper, and a quantity of graphic illustrations such as lithographs, etchings, and other works in these media to which he added techniques of his own invention. He cast the many plasters referred to, made four or five large new bronzes (Plate 130) and perhaps a dozen small ones, also about six or eight new plasters and clay portraits, some of which he also cast. Then, in the continuing overflow of energy and ideas so characteristic of him, he made at random an uncounted number of small souvenir objects. These consist of paper cutouts, objects of torn paper, folded paper, bent wire, and tinfoil, as well as those made from bristles, matches, string, and other materials casually found at hand. He contrived also two small bas-relief cardboard cutouts sewn instead of pasted on cardboard, and then painted, a combination of *collage* and construction (Plate 129, top shelf). In addition he wrote a six-act play (1941), and designed a curtain for the ballet (1945).

Picasso painted all manner of subjects: portraits of friends and strangers; the several versions of the famous tomato plant that grew in a pot on his studio window sill and bore fruit that must have seemed a great delicacy during the war. He painted a large political theme, successor to the *Guernica*, called *The Charnel House;* also many views of Notre Dame and the Seine, views from his studio window, views in Royan, a large variety of still lifes, and quantities of portraits and figure groups; tauromachy and other animal pictures. Finally, he painted the *Kissers* series which precedes a huge work planned, the title for which will be *Le Vert-Galant.* Two canvases of the setting itself have already been painted. The large work when complete will combine many figures with this Seine scene, a twentieth-century version of the idea of the *Grande Jatte.*

6

This listing of cold statistics, though impressive, is even more so in view of the fierce energy and challenging imagery that are to be found in the work itself. To have accomplished such results in the midst of an environment so disruptive to the spirit must have been a herculean task of concentration and will, especially since the eventual fate of Picasso's *Shrecklichkammer* (Chamber of Horrors) art, if it fell into the hands of the Nazi culture machine, would have been highly questionable. No less chilling to the spirit than to the marrow of the bones was the notorious cold of the unheated occupation winters. The long food lines of Paris (still in existence more than a year after the liberation), the gray bread that looks and tastes like sawdust, indicate that the conditions there during the early forties could easily have depressed creative will to the point of non-existence. High moral courage was needed, and this was shown outstandingly by Picasso in artistic creation, but it was shared in no small degree by the equally underfed but more suppressed man on the street who saved from his scanty food allotments and hoarded his precious liquor against the day when he might ultimately fete the liberating forces. Thus Picasso, himself a formidable will, could—for the very reason that he continued so implacably to be the painter he had always been—emerge out of war as much a symbol of undefeated democracy as did the fighting Partisans themselves.

It is not necessary to paint a man with a gun.
An apple can be just as revolutionary.
PABLO PICASSO, March 1946.

T HIS REMARK, made while discussing the Art and Resistance Exhibition, in Paris, reflects Picasso's lifelong attitude toward art, that subject matter, however important in itself, is merely a point of departure to a truly revolutionary artist. What is said in the visual language of paint is more significant and less dated than literal subject matter, which carries conviction only in proportion to the extent to which it has been evolved into the timeless communication of inventive pictorial ideas.

Almost the first news of Picasso after the liberation was the announcement that he had joined the Communist party. This was amplified by his own statement that he had taken this action because he had found the Communists to be the bravest among his Resistance companions. This was electrifying news to people of all convictions, including the Communists themselves, who were overwhelmed with the importance of being able to add to their ranks the key figure of the twentieth-century renaissance in art.

The question of whether or not some new aesthetic direction would carry him away from that which he had maintained throughout his dynamic career became an issue whose outcome the entire art community in the English-speaking world awaited with great curiosity. Picasso had always been a revolutionary in art, independent, courageous, and totally uncompromising. There is ample evidence that many socially conscious artists in this country reject the intellectual experimentation on which our culture, paralleling our science, has thrived, and tend, after their conversion, to concentrate on the narrative aspects of propagandistic subject matter set forth, usually, in terms of a more conservative aesthetic.

On the basis of this precedent, the question, "What will Picasso do now?" appeared to involve the alternatives of his consistently continuing creativity or his possible neglect of pure aesthetic contributions for proselytizing. Would he use his great talents on a plane so intensive, concentrated, and advanced that they would continue to furnish, as they had done for so many years, principles and ideas to inspire the generations of artists to come? Or would he use them for painting propaganda in such a manner as to allow his aesthetics to conform to conservative standards, as a compromise to the assumed taste of the layman?

Picasso has answered the question by remaining as clearly consistent in his direction as the scientist whose province is pure research rather than the specific practical applications of his findings. At the same time, Picasso is no novice at painting pictures with latent or direct social content. The emaciated underprivileged world of his Blue Period (1901–04); the pre-World War II series of incisive etchings titled *Dreams and Lies of Franco;* his great anti-Franco painting *Guernica* with its accompanying group of some sixty-five vigorously stated preliminary and post-facto paintings, drawings, and sketches; and during War II his *The Charnel House,* all are social in theme. Besides these, there are also the drawings during the war of the bullfight which he often invested with a symbolic-political meaning. Finally, in 1945, he drew a portrait of Maurice Thorez, secretary of the Communist party in France. Yet, despite the fact that he returns at times, even if for a single picture, such as that of M. Thorez, to a more representational and less disturbing realist manner, the aesthetic treatment in these becomes progressively more advanced through the years. His new political affiliations have not deterred or changed the course of his pictorial progress, nor have they accelerated it. The pictures of this new period merely constitute part of his endless choice of material, and the aesthetic handling of social subjects follows the general trends of his work. As he breaks new paths and penetrates deeper into plastic principles and ideas, the pictorial language becomes more aggressively original and upsetting to established habits, and increasingly difficult, perhaps, to accept without a very special effort at understanding.

This is particularly true of his paintings of the war years, in which all of his tendencies reach a new peak or climax. Because of the extreme deformation of recognizable elements of representation, especially those of the human face and figure, Picasso's painting is perhaps even further removed from general sympathy than pure geometric abstraction, which his work is not.

If social content, instead of more traditional subjects, is the basis of Picasso's painting, this content finds a counterpart in an aesthetic, and also in ideas (generally symbolic), that give validity to its use. This artist uses a wide latitude of expressiveness; as pointed out, his presentation of a social theme is oriented to the respective phase of his work in which it appears. No aesthetic compromise is involved. The artist, on the contrary, invariably forces the observer to sharpen his own aesthetic awareness.

The value of Picasso's contribution to art lies in his insistent utilization of the full power of his own gifts. He works through to the most profound levels he can reach, for it is true of him, as of all artists, that in proportion to the extent he penetrates into the core of a problem does he elevate the achievement. In this way, whatever the material he uses as a point of departure, he discovers in it a significant visual imagery. If he takes from the environment it will be either direct subject matter, or indirectly, he will use the subtle and elusive ideas that influence him from the world at large and the times in which he lives. If these factors seem at times intangible and remote, they may, nevertheless, be doubly important as the nucleus of future ideas and directions. Then, at a time when the more obvious styles of contemporary painting shall have become obsolete, these factors will exert their greatest social force.

The *de Stijl* Group of Holland (organized in 1917), whose ideas, like those of all advanced trends today, originated in cubism, has already exerted great influence, and within a comparatively short time. *De Stijl's* leading painter, Mondrian, in his two-dimensional geometric arrangements of space and line in their limited range of primary colors, translated as they have been into modern architecture, has had a more direct effect on our standards of living than literal representations of slum homes. Mondrian and the *de Stijl* Group are almost solely responsible for the contemporary concept of the uncluttered household with its simple, clean, utile furniture, as well as for revolutionary changes in architecture, with an orientation to sunlight and air, modern equipment, ample living space, inclusion of recreational and educational facilities for adults as well as children. This is no more than a transference of principles from the machine, through the artist—or series of artists—who form the sensitive intermediary, and, completing the cycle, eventually back into life itself.

Picasso's contribution, then, from the standpoint of the sociological, is characteristically personal. According to his own statement heading this chapter, he considers his art generically revolutionary, and continues unremittingly along the lines of his lifelong aesthetic convictions. A change in the direction of his art is uncalled for; the basic integrity of his work and theories is the guiding principle of his artistic history. The very prestige of Picasso is almost solely due to his perseverant, experimental widening of the horizons of art, and, concomitantly, he is a greater conquest than any other living artist to the side of his new political confreres.

For the very reason that he has maintained his personal direction on the highest creative level of which he is capable, and has striven continually to surpass his previous accomplishments, his work has at the same time increased in material value. It is argued by some that this commercial rise is the result of planned publicity, a conspiracy on the part of the French dealers, even of the French Government. It is hard to imagine a more difficult product to exploit for this purpose than the work of Picasso. Apart from aesthetic considerations, which should be, after all, the main ones, the wide acceptance of his art during his lifetime may perhaps be due in no little measure to the fact that we are today trying to avoid a repetition of the belated recognition which came to the artists of the late nineteenth century. Such artists as Seurat, Van Gogh, Cézanne, and Henri Rousseau died unacclaimed except by a limited group of intellectuals, and the dramatic circumstances of their neglect have been highly publicized ever since. This acclaim to a living artist predicates the assumption of responsibility on the part of the art-conscious public toward even a revolutionary artist in their time—an important indication of the widespread cognizance of art today.

For many years Picasso's practice has been to contribute his paintings to social causes. Recently in one week alone he donated four paintings: *The Charnel House* (Plate 16), his major picture of the war years,[1] and three large still lifes (Plates 28, 33, 65). The latter were immediately sold for the benefit of Spanish Refugee Relief. These are only a few of the many contributions he makes periodically to organizations with which he is in sympathy.

Some Left-wing writers, at least in the English-speaking countries, who previously stigmatized Picasso as a charlatan and denounced his art as decadent, have recently reversed themselves and have now become his apologists. This change of opinion would be more encouraging aesthetically if it were based either on a change in Picasso's work favorable to their point of view or a fuller understanding of it as it has always existed, but it is unfortunately only too often due to his recent political affiliation. On the other hand, when some of his previous supporters now take the position that his art has become so difficult as to be completely beyond comprehension, this judgment is all too apt to proceed only from their repugnance to his new political convictions.

That the war had a great effect upon Picasso as a person with a

---

[1]Picasso gave this painting, although unfinished, at the request of the Art and Resistance organization, who featured it in their show in Paris, February 1946. They agreed not to offer it for sale until after it could be finished by Picasso.

deeply felt sense of social responsibility is self-evident. An examination of his canvases chronologically will show its strong influence upon the mood and temper of his work, but far from diverting him, this kept him fervently pursuing the uncompromising aesthetic standards maintained throughout his career. Even including the painting *The Charnel House*, there was no direct use of social theme, but much symbolic overtone, such as in the use of skulls and of the common leek as well as the paintings of helmetlike death heads done in Royan in 1940. A check of dates of his canvases, however, gives no inkling of battles won or lost, of the Allied invasion, liberation, or final victory. For example, during the Battle of the Streets preceding the liberation, despite the shooting that pockmarked neighboring houses, Picasso was busy painting a gouache after Poussin and a portrait of his daughter, Conchita (Plates 99, 100).

His work during the war runs the gamut from deepest melancholy to elation, and it is in its over-all affective character rather than in specific reportage that it reflects the tensions and violence of the war years. In a statement issued at the time he joined the Communist party, Picasso said: "Through design and color I have tried to penetrate deeper into a knowledge of the world and of men, so that this knowledge might free us. In my own way, I have always said what I considered most true, most just, and best, and therefore most beautiful . . ."

AN ARTIST, well known for his excessive desire for recognition and one jump ahead of the Germans in their advance through France, finally got to Royan where Picasso had been living. Meeting Picasso on the street, he excitedly asked: "With the Germans right on our heels, what are we to do?" Picasso replied with customary humor: "Make exhibitions!"

During the long years of the occupation, Picasso, confining himself to his Paris studio, showed his paintings only to closest friends. His first public showing after the war came in the fall of 1944, when he participated in the Exposition de la Liberation at the Salon d'Automne. The Salon, following its practice of featuring an artist at each year's exhibit, designated Picasso for this honor, an entire section being devoted to his art. This equivalent of a huge one-man exhibit included seventy-three paintings and four pieces of sculpture done between 1937 and 1944, and constituted almost a third of the total number of paintings hung.

The Salon had correctly anticipated that a large portion of the art public should be keenly interested in seeing the work Picasso had done in the war years. That some part would consist of "Picassophobes" was inevitable. The public which attended constituted those who have gone along with Picasso in the long and arduous journey of his difficult but highly rewarding art; recent converts and new companions of his newly announced political affiliations; those who follow events out of mere curiosity; and, finally, noisy and demonstrative opposition which is the invariable French accompaniment to the presentation of progressive ideas and activities in the arts.

This last group proved more than ordinarily unruly at the Salon show, and the extensive repercussions reached even the lay public.

14

Although Picasso has a wide following in Paris, he was almost unknown there to the man on the street. To a large section of the American public that has long been aware of Picasso and has availed itself of many opportunities to appraise the large and important exhibits, some nationally circulated, this fact may come as a surprise.

That the lay public in Paris attended at all was due in no small measure to the excitement caused by the artistically and politically reactionary elements. Their protests and angry meetings were played up by the newspapers, and as a result exhibit attendance skyrocketed. The desirability of this type of publicity is dubious; still the value of publicity lies in the interest developed. Moreover, partisanship often clarifies issues and introduces many observers to fields of new visual experience.

The reactionary group demonstrated agitatedly and derisively before Picasso's paintings at the Salon. On one occasion they attacked the pictures, removing fifteen from the walls before the guards could intercede. When the disturbance had been put down, the canvases, undamaged, were rehung and no further incidents occurred at the Salon. But the younger demonstrators, mostly students from the Sorbonne, rushed to Picasso's studio in the Rue des Grands Augustines, and, holding a protest meeting in the courtyard, demanded the burning of Picasso's work. Few gendarmes were to be found in Paris at this time, consequently the students were not dispersed. After an unsuccessful attempt to break into the premises—the studio is on the upper floor—the troublemakers moodily departed.

This hysterical outburst was, in the final analysis, the extreme reaction to the impact of the paintings themselves. The intervening years since Picasso's last exhibit, filled with strain of war, humiliation of quick defeat, indignity of living under alien domination, bitter resentment against collaboration, had left their mark. Picasso's work being, if anything, more tortured, more agonized than ever before, more furiously animalistic, rebellious, and violent, it was converted into a convenient object for the release of constricting public tensions.

The frequent showings of Picasso's work, which had to some degree familiarized the public with the progressive steps in his remarkably rapid but always consistent evolution, had not taken place during these years. The art public thus found itself obliged to make too sudden a transition, to face a *fait accompli* of overwhelming power. The assault upon the emotions by Picasso's work in the original (markedly more acute than in reproduction) was too massive to be borne. Startlingly vivid color is generally accompanied by vigorous and profuse brushing in of paint; or, when monotones are used, these suffuse the observer with melancholy. There is no respite from the attack upon the emotions and the senses in any of these pictures. The dying horse of *Guernica*, which had seemed frighteningly intense at the time, seems considerably milder by comparison.

Whatever reproductions of new works had appeared outside the reach of German censorship, that is, through Underground presses in occupied Paris, had appeared only in a few books and magazines of limited circulation. Consequently they effected little or no public preparation for the work now to be seen at the Salon.

The student demonstrators, having grown up in the war period, had been subjected to a virtual cultural blackout. These young people, when faced with modern works of art which were in actuality transmutations from experiences in their daily environment, seemed to reject completely the validity of their experiences. Still, these very experiences obtained in the violence and brutality of the war which surrounded them, in the perennially present aesthetic of machine forms and rhythms, and in the wide use of functional design in advertising layout, packaging, furniture, fabrics, and household articles, which owe their very modernity to advance-guard art. To comprehend Picasso's recent paintings demanded more of them than they were prepared or equipped to give, psychologically or otherwise. Weary of conflicts and insecurity, they were in no frame of mind to accept revolutionary concepts in art.

It may perhaps be argued, furthermore, that there is a vast appetite on the part of the public for the mediocre in art. Anything that is unfamiliar, that asks of the observer a reappraisal of values, that requires active rather than passive participation, is anathema. Yet this spiritual laziness often exerts far more energy in maintaining its defenses than would be needed to investigate the validity of new ideas in art.

A little story illustrating this lethargy furnished Picasso with an opportunity for one of his quick and witty thrusts. A conservative-minded editor, visiting Pierre Loeb's studio, remarked: "I think modern painters go too far—they exaggerate too much. Just today I saw a simple outline sketch signed by Matisse, and for this people pay exorbitant prices. That is going too far." Picasso, who had been sitting by reading, calmly replied that for Matisse to achieve that single line took fifty years of concentrated study and hard work. The editor, at once sensing his disadvantage, tried to retreat, by saying hastily: "Oh, I know little about art, I am a peasant." "Oh," Picasso shot back, "so you're a peasant. Let's talk your language! Have you got eggs? Have you got butter?"

Among the anti-Picasso demonstrators were also to be found the dissenters who had formed a cultural opposition through political indoctrination, and beyond these were the ever-present aesthetic reactionaries, those cultural Pharisees who, living solely in the past, pass judgment on the new values of contemporary art through the obsolescence of their own viewpoints. Even some of the hitherto ardent supporters of Picasso found this new phase difficult to accept upon first viewing.

The general effect of this exhibition was as hysterical as had been the New York showing thirty-one years earlier of the cubist pictures of Picasso, together with other vanguard art, at the Armory Show. Everyone interested in progressive ideas in art is familiar with the inevitable adverse criticism and lack of understanding that accompany the first opening of new paths. The attacks upon the impressionists are a familiar part of art history, and even further in the past one finds these manifestations of resistance wherever there was a radical departure from the well-worn, familiar directions. Not more than fifty years ago and over two hundred years after they were painted, El Greco's long-neglected pictures met with the following comment of unknown origin: "Through heavy nightmares he seems to guide his brush, revealing the twisted incubus of his heated brain."[1] This is the typical reaction of unadaptive persons young or old, unable or unwilling to abandon their visual and emotional conditioning. On the other hand, it augurs well for the vital, creative progress of an artist, if, after having shaken to the core the smug Philistines of 1913 in America, he can, by new phases, arouse reaction, as late as 1944 in France, the birthplace of modern art.

Apart from single examples of Picasso's late work, shown in various exhibits—in most instances paintings which he had donated to raise money for relief purposes—his first one-man show in a gallery was held at Galerie Louis Carré in June 1945.[2] Resentment of Picasso's political affiliations was expressed by some of the potential purchasers—a new objection related in no way to art appreciation.

Late in December 1945 an exhibition that was to prove even a greater storm center than the Salon d'Automne show opened at the Victoria and Albert Museum in London. Entitled *Picasso-Matisse*, it included twenty-five examples by Picasso (1939–45) and thirty by Matisse (1896–1944), and was arranged by L'Association Française d'Action Artistique and the British Council, two official government groups invested with the task of establishing a cultural exchange between France and England. Government sponsored, the exhibition attracted a full cross section of the public. That official sponsorship

---

[1] Such a comment, if made today, might—in the light of discoveries in psychology, the unconscious mind, and automatism—easily be construed as a sympathetic understanding of the functions of the unconscious in the creative process.

[2] At the time of writing, the second annual exhibition of the paintings of Picasso opens at this gallery, (Plates 127, 128).

should be given to such revolutionary forms of art was almost unheard of, and the selection of paintings, involving as it did progressive standards of taste, inevitably provoked a controversy in England.

The Matisse paintings were to some degree retrospective, including many handsome works, but the Picasso paintings proved to be the magnet that drew the throngs. Dating from his most fierce and embattled phase, 1939 to 1945, they provoked vehement attack. British response, typically more restrained than the French, took a form quite different from the physical manifestations of Gallic protest. Apart from the soapbox outburst of one woman, who suddenly addressed the gallery visitors with a heated speech, there was no specific demonstration. Still, the cumulative effect of opinions was tantamount to a mass demonstration.

The newspapers and magazine reviews aided considerably in sustaining the charged atmosphere of the controversy. These gave large and continued space to the exhibit, airing the usual dogmatic, reactionary points of view, but publishing also many intelligent and literate reviews, while devoting, as well, much space to reproduction. The impassioned exchanges of opinion that took place freely and openly before the pictures formed the basis of colorful news articles by roving reporters, and revealed the points of view of persons of all tastes and degrees of knowledgeability. Even the comments of children were printed. Numerous letters to the papers supplemented the serious and logical reviews as well as the derisive and emotional ones. It is clearly indicative of general lay interest that the majority of the students visiting the exhibit in England were favorably inclined; in France they were hostile and reactionary. In spite of many letter writers who urged that the show be closed, attendance was so large and interest so great that the exhibit, originally scheduled to run from December 5 to 29, was extended to January 15, 1946. Not since the post-impressionist show arranged by Roger Fry in 1910 had there been an exhibition so disturbing yet healthily stimulating to the public.

The vital issues included aesthetics, ideologies, and education. There was the usual bigoted attitude toward genuinely creative art. Some artists shared this view, either from aesthetic obtuseness or from a need to protect their commercial security by rejecting anything outside the limited scope of their own personal methods. These called the exhibit rubbish, said the pictures had been painted as a hoax, or made aggressive demands to have them explained, with apparently no attempt to understand. Not the least of the offenders were, as among the French, those who found it degenerate because, they said, it reflected degenerate times. Subjecting themselves most severely to ridicule were those protesting on the basis of the alleged corruptive influence of Picasso's painting upon the young. Little or none of the adverse criticism was stirred, as it was in France, by the political issue of Picasso's recent entry into the Communist party.

On the other side, there was much thoughtful evaluation of Picasso's work. The public was asked to approach it with a receptive mind, free from prejudice and, as far as possible, from the limiting preconceptions of antithetic visual experience. It was presented for what, after more than thirty-five years, it still is—the vanguard of ideas in contemporary art. The position of the artist as creator of new worlds was stressed, as well as the fact that reality is better understood when pointed up by the penetrating perception of the creative artist. There was special and repeated emphasis on Picasso's work from the standpoint of its emotional content and the spiritual energy and forcefulness that had gone into its making, and on the characteristic and traditional Spanish violence with which he had been expressing his humanely grounded fury over the cruelties of a world at war. From the plastic approach, the points were reiterated that the double-eyed profile in Picasso's paintings derived from medieval Catalonian wall paintings, and that some of his images were inspired by Spanish early Renaissance polychrome statues of Christ, strong arguments in a tradition-revering England.

To establish precedent, the controversy over the showing of Cézanne and the post-impressionists in 1910 was referred to, with the comment that the writers of the most violent diatribes against that exhibit were today lost in obscurity, while the paintings themselves lived on as masterpieces.

Although the ridiculed post-impressionist has been acclaimed a master in the passing years, it does not necessarily follow that a ridiculed artist of a later date need also eventually be acclaimed. But time is unquestionably important in conditioning one's acceptance of revolutionary art forms. *Guernica,* for example (though not in the exhibition), was referred to by most reviewers as a masterpiece, though when shown for the first time at Burlington House only seven years before, in 1938, many of the same writers had roundly condemned it.

A little later, back across the Channel, the same type of argument formed the introduction to the second of Abbé Morel's lectures on Picasso given at the Sorbonne. Held on February 15, 1946, a month after the closing of the London show, it was a repeat performance of a lecture that had been delivered shortly before, and was planned to accommodate the large overflow which failed to gain admission at the first. However, getting in was quite as great a task at the second, for although the hall holds some 3,000 people, every tribunal was crowded with standees. The priest, a great admirer of the work of Picasso, began by recalling that Ingres, Delacroix, Courbet, Corot, Cézanne, and Van Gogh all had been severely criticized and misunderstood during their lifetime. He quoted from writing of the period to prove the point, and then used this to impugn those who today so arbitrarily reject Picasso's paintings.

The abbé continued his lecture with a series of slides of various periods. A simple outline drawing of a boy's head of the Blue Period was greeted by the most prolonged applause of the whole lecture. This indicated that even in Paris this early period, not Picasso's most profound, is, because of its ready intelligibility, still the most popular. Yet this very popularity has been precipitated in no small way by the importance of his succeeding, and difficult, work.

When a 1907 masklike head of his Negroid Period was shown, the audience broke out in derision. As observed, the most controversial reactions are produced by Picasso's inventions based upon the human form, which seem to antagonize public sentiment to a far greater degree than his equally abstract and reconstructed imagery of still life, landscape, or animals. An African wood sculpture next appeared on the screen, whereupon a large part of the audience, believing it to be another work by Picasso, again voiced disapproval. When the abbé cleared up the point, quiet was quickly, almost shamefacedly, restored.

Two hours of lecture was continually interrupted by derisive comment from the audience. As at the Salon, the majority of the lecture audience came—and paid the price of admission—not for enlightenment, but for the personal purpose of giving vent to their own heated antagonisms.

Not that the lecturer was subjected only to caustic heckling. Some interruptions were rather more humorous. Near the conclusion of the talk a series of recent drawings were shown giving variations on the taurine form. The series began with a robust, full-bodied bull which, through the simplification of line and form, gradually became a mere skeletal outline. When the final one was projected—the steer's head was now reduced almost to a pin point—a brief lull ensued during which a burly voice from the balcony shouted pithily: "Now I know why there's a meat shortage!"

In a similar vein a cartoon recently appeared in the Paris press lampooning Picasso. Placed next to a reproduction of a minotaur by Picasso, the cartoon showed a bull asking the concierge to see Picasso. "It's personal," he added.

Countering shallow diatribes is the genuine appreciation of poets, writers, artists, collectors, and others, who, wherever possible, give moral and spiritual support to the painter. It is nevertheless evident from his life-long work that Picasso's real spiritual sustenance comes from within himself, from the drive that has made possible the almost incredible volume and variety of work he has accomplished.

22

Picasso epitomizes in his own person the tyrannous urge of our time to create. Through him, this urge—still triumphant—comes back to numbers of other artists, giving them new conviction and the nourishing ideas from which to grow. The many brilliant artists living today work the more spiritedly because he constantly discovers and lays bare the real spiritual issues of our time. Distortion and angularity, so characteristic of his paintings, far from willful, are the inevitable expression of the reaction of a powerful, clear-seeing, fearless personality to the scientific and aesthetic character and the philosophic meaning implicit in life today. Surcharging and clearing the cultural atmosphere, his revolutionary achievements become the outward manifestations of a powerful drive, incalculable in its effect upon the vitality of art as well as upon the general awareness of it in our day. For Picasso has electrified, not only his immediate environment, but the cultural centers of the world with a dynamic, revitalizing energy and a passionate contemporaneity of vision. Coming from the true inwardness of his own nature, these are, in their sum, fecundating forces that, on their outer fringes of influence, have become so universal as at times no longer to be even associated with his personality or his name.

PICASSO seems at one time or other in his career to have covered almost everything within the scope of human experience. Such is the compass of his perception that if one were able thoroughly to study his creative processes, one would come to know virtually all of the ramifications of these in man. Extraordinarily active in connection with the huge creative gestation of this gigantic figure is the process of self-renewal that goes on so unabatedly and at so high a pitch that there seems no end to the flow of ideas or the extent of productivity. Actually, there are stretches of time, sometimes months, in which he does no painting whatever. Even then, however, the preliminary stages leading to pictorial invention are at work within him. Apart from the myriad "souvenir" objects already referred to, which he is constantly making from any material that happens to be at hand, he is filling himself incessantly with the experiences that become the substance of his work. Life is the field for the most penetratingly observed records of seen experience and the unseen relations—to be visually interpreted later—between persons, places, and things. Works of art from every civilization furnish the endless suggestions and correspondences, fitted to the present, that Picasso's gargantuan appetite requires. For this latter reason his work is thought to border occasionally on the encyclopedic, and this might be so were it not for his complete reconversion of material and re-emphasis of ideas. He needs both life and art, and these in great quantity and intensity, to keep his creativity perpetually fecund.

It is Picasso's contention that the artist, after working for many years toward ever-widening horizons, experiences increasing difficulty to achieve and to retain fresh artistic awareness. It is clear, however, that he himself has maintained inspiration continually at the thresh-

24

old of initial impulse for almost fifty years—a protean achievement requiring the most vigilant, sensitive, and intuitive nurturing and protection of the creative process. By keeping faith with the individuality of vision that is his artistic birthright, he has avoided the stylistic formalization that causes many an artist to repeat himself rather than to grow to his own full artistic stature. All through his painting career, by rejecting flattering commissions, by refusing to repeat or to plagiarize himself, Picasso has turned his back on easy success. That in so doing he has achieved wide recognition and a large financial success is another matter.

VARIATION   Rejecting repetition, Picasso fully embraces the laws of variation. He seems, indeed, as versatile as nature itself. Starting a theme, he brings it to life in an almost mathematical multiplication of its varied expressive potentialities. In this he is virtually the equivalent of nature, an autonomous fusion of many elements, one that creates prolifically, lavishly, and in so many basic combinations that the results seem at times to be complete mutations rather than variations.

The complex level on which he functions is demonstrated in his work of the war years. Since, because of government restrictions on the export of art, so many of his paintings of this period remained in Paris, a broad representation was available there for study.

A quick chronological survey gives the impression that he has gone rapidly from one manner of expression to another. This has often been a mistaken criticism of Picasso's work. However, closer observation discloses a definite developmental order. The half-length figures, for instance, can be divided into groups, each of which shows a continuity of transition from naturalism—relatively speaking—to abstract or surrealist invention. One group of figures is markedly angular (Plates 85 to 87); another is characterized by a flowing or curvilinear design (Plates 79 to 84) that is Spanish and at the same time spiritually similar in its sparseness and extreme simplification to work of the early New England itinerant portraitists. Still another group of figure paintings consists of the twisting and displacement of more or less realistic faces and figures in a manner that transforms them into magical and surreal icons (Plates 94 to 98). These are only a few of the many tendencies to be found in his recent paintings.

The artistic continuities in the different types by no means, however, follow a chronological sequence. Picasso does not necessarily move, that is to say, in sequential steps from realism toward abstraction. He may make a highly abstract version of figure or still life at one date, and follow with a quite representational variation on the same theme at a later date. Interspersed are numerous subjects: half-length and full-figure pieces, figure groups, the Paris scenes, and various series of still lifes, animals, and others. Each of these, too, has pictorially related psychological content and emotional stress. So intricate and complex a network, or mental pattern, is suggested by the many dynamic directions and subjects that the whole body of work constitutes an amazing—almost superhuman—achievement.

Statistics on the huge productivity of this artist have been given earlier in the text, but it might be of interest to add here that Picasso has in his possession dozens of large portfolios filled with the oil sketches on paper he made during the war. These notes, often quite fully articulated, were done while working on easel painting. It is his habit to turn away from his canvas, continuing to paint, usually in blacks or *grisaille*. He generally makes several of these sketches a day, of which he says: "The accumulation of pictorial ideas on paper eventually adds up to something I can use on the canvas. Although," he adds, "these never come out the same." Implied here is the fact that his free motor activity furnishes spontaneous images and ideas. This is a method akin to the automatism of surrealist artists.

Contrary to popular belief, Picasso is not and has never been a nonfigurative painter, as he always uses subject matter (objects) as a starting point. Although reconverted through his own invention, these objects still retain their essential identity, remaining distinguishable painted images: a vase, a bottle, a table, a mirror, a person.

Picasso's use of literal elements of realism may be confirmed by examining, for example, *Still Life with Skull and Leeks* (Plate 63),

OBJECT AS A POINT OF DEPARTURE

which, surprisingly, so confused several editors that it was reproduced wrong side up in at least two foreign publications. In this painting, clearly recognizable, skull and pitcher face each other; some leeks lie across the front of the table. Attached to the french window in the background is a peg-shaped handle, which, rather abstractly rendered here, may be observed more realistically in *Tomato Plant Before the Window* (Plate 29). The octagonal tiles of the floor may be verified in the photograph of Picasso's studio (Plate 41). Clearly discernible in the foreground of the painting are the four legs of the table; the shadows thrown by the table, combined with the lines of the table top and legs, form a facet-shaped construction. Lines of light as well as of shadow, together with defining lines such as those of the corner of the room and sides of the window, form the structure and establish tensions within the picture. No line or shape to be found here is an arbitrary departure from nature, not even that of light or of shadow. All belong intrinsically to the observable aspects of the objects themselves. The difference between commonly accepted realism and the realism projected by this painting lies, aside from any consideration of the picture's plastic validity, in the poetic and psychological transposition of subject matter.

Although Picasso constantly works toward uncommonplace vision, he reverts occasionally to a more naturalistic reality, reapproaching the point of departure as if to refresh his seeing, to discover anew and develop the discoveries. That the naturalism of any creative artist exists only to a limited degree on canvas is a fact frequently overlooked. Perfection of naturalistic form is a convention belonging to classic Greece, and to a lesser degree, to the Renaissance. Today's realism lies elsewhere. At one end, as if belonging to yesterday, is the unimaginative academic point of view; in the middle are found familiar techniques and styles of representation which are so often used for purposes of description; at the ultimate frontiers, and truly contemporaneous, are to be found the abstract concepts and poetic imagery whose advanced nature requires the highest imagination.

A fundamental method employed by Picasso for achieving variation is that commonly called distortion. Distortion in form was originally, and still is to a large degree, dictated by the attempt to reconcile the psychological factors of inner and outer vision to the true physical law of the canvas: to convert what is seen through the eye, the sensibility and the experience of the artist, into terms consistent with two-dimensional concepts. This device may or may not result in comparative abstraction of design; it does aid in bringing about in aesthetic terms of contemporary validity a legitimate and convincing intensification of the realistic qualities of the objects depicted.

In his portraits, no matter how far removed they may be from photographic likeness, the head and all of the features, however reshaped and displaced, are invariably present. On a face the eyes may be horizontal and vertical respectively, and these may either be presented on the same profile, or opposite profiles may be designated for the nose and for the mouth. These, again, may be transformed into masks or skulls, and sometimes into both, but invariably all of the facial features will be indicated. The displacements, having psychological as well as plastic value, create a diverse and keenly observed portrait of the personality. "Portraits should possess," in the words of Picasso, "not physical, not spiritual, but psychological likeness."

Reproductions of six progressively abstract portraits of Miss Dora Maar (Plates 48 to 53) show how the artist alters his approach to his subject, retaining the essential resemblance to the original model, but also conveying in varying degrees of subtlety and penetration a representation of the qualities of outer composure and inner intensity which are so characteristic of Miss Maar as a person.

It should be borne in mind that the displacements in Picasso's recent portrayals are similar to those appearing in his cubist portraits. However, the cubist examples were obscured by extensive division or breakdown of the forms into geometric plane surfaces, and the diffusion created by the use of an impressionist brush stroke. In the portraits of the 1940s, where so much of the representational aspect of objects is retained, the displacements seem much more startling, like actual physical deformities.

The distortions and displacements of human features are disquieting, authentic as they may be in their aesthetic fitness and psychological verity. It is obvious that the extent and special quality of horror in this new phase were at least heightened and their advent quickened by war. In this respect these paintings stem from *Guernica*, and, just as war itself had spread from the localized Spanish conflict to all-consuming world-wide warfare, these distortions, magnified, extend into a whole new phase of his painting. That many canvases of the war period express an underlying calm and quiet really proves this. They represent not only different aspects of one of the most complex personalities of our time but, in this context, his own ambivalent reaction to violence.

Inasmuch as new phases in the work of a creative personality, no matter how suddenly they may appear or how apparently they may be inspired by outward events, still relate to his whole prior course of development, so this new phase in Picasso can be traced back to the cubism he himself had so largely initiated and developed. In cubism, of course, displacement arose technically from the use of the circulating viewpoint which permitted the painter to observe the three-dimensional object simultaneously from several points of view and to present these various aspects two-dimensionally on the surface of the canvas.

SIMULTANEITY, OR THE CIRCU- LATING VIEW- POINT, TODAY

By painting several sides of an object (circulating viewpoint) and placing them side by side like flattened-out sides of a box (two-dimensional presentation), the cubist was able, for example, to paint the belly, sides, and back of a guitar, all juxtaposed. Further to stress the surface plane of the canvas, the oil technique was extended by pasting into the composition cutouts of paper and other flat materials (*papier collé* and *collage*). Since 1909 the circulating viewpoint, together with the technique for visualizing this (translating three-dimensional objects into terms of the two-dimensional picture plane), has been inseparable in the work of Picasso. The cubist technique remains valid today, and the displacement and rearrangement of the anatomy of objects and persons (particularly faces) found in the paintings of the war years stem directly from cubist sources, although the manner and spirit in which they are now used differ, in ways and for reasons under discussion, profoundly from his earlier periods.

In several 1940–42 studies of a sleeping nude (Plate 70) Picasso carries the idea of the circulating viewpoint further than ever before, presenting three views side by side: part of the front, the back, and the other part of the front again, as if the figure were in rotation.

The pictures of recent years again point up the fact that Picasso was the prime mover of cubism. His consistently profound and repeated use of the principles of cubism throughout his career, and, more than ever in the years of World War II, indicates that these principles were essentially formulated by him as a true expression of his own basic personality. The originality with which he has recast these concepts at intervals is proof of a continued reorientation to those fundamentals which were articulated so sensitively and intuitively in analytical cubism (1909–12), and with increasing clarity and power ever since.

Preferring a variety of lightings, Picasso paints under the most varying conditions, in the glare of the sun (his studio has no top lighting), at twilight or midnight, by candle, lamp, or electricity. He externalizes also what might be called his own inner vision, doing this abstractly, in terms of his own special concepts pertaining to physical light. From cubist beginnings it has been a guiding principle with him, while giving the outer aspect and underlying structure of objects, to show also how they vary in themselves and in their effect upon each other in space under the play of light. This light is not fixed, but comes from two or more directions, frequently following the viewpoint as it circulates about the object, and often giving the feeling of this movement as well. Although modeling, or chiaroscuro, has been reintroduced in some of his recent pictures (for reasons we shall see), he has, for the most part, delineated light, as he has done over the years since *collage,* with incisive sharpness. He breaks it up prismatically, obtaining thereby an endless number of angular facets as well as

LIGHT AND ITS EFFECT ON LINE, FORM, AND COLOR

precisely contoured pattern formations which, while at great variance with habitual seeing, are intrinsically even more real. This prismatic representation of light is demonstrated with particular clarity in the Paris scenes (Plates 43, 44), where the facet construction of the picture depends upon the action of light and shade on the buildings, the bridges across the Seine, and the river itself.

Light, too, has its effect upon color. Throughout his work, color, which does not necessarily agree with nature, may become even more divergent and kaleidoscopic under the effect of light (Plate 81).

Furthermore, light and dark, while opposites, possess equally positive properties; shadows are treated, not passively as the absence of light, but are given the attributes of independent, active agents.

Using greatly varying conditions, the artist is able to isolate, with the aid of his highly developed visual and imaginative powers, all manner of fascinating phenomena of the behavior of form under light. This factor, considered with others: the wide use of plane surfaces which even his use of modeling must serve (two-dimensionality) and displacement (contemporary version of the circulating viewpoint), are largely responsible for the extremely individual transmutations in his work. These, together with the play of his personal poetry and intellect upon the subject matter, account for the long step between the subject in its literal appearance and the new representation he ultimately makes.

The modeling which reappears to some extent in a number of recent pictures is not a retrogression, but, on the contrary, another step forward, for rather than an end in itself it is another means for enriching creative possibilities. This is especially true in the portraits (Plates 96, 97), where modeling becomes a technique for shock when the natural object is lifted out of context and placed into new and unexpected relationships.

EQUILIBRIUM   Precarious equilibrium is perhaps the most basic and enduring quality, and the most breath-taking, in Picasso's work. In observing this in operation, one can almost conclude that all of his ideas derive from the manipulation—like that of an engineer—of forms and color to create the delicately poised systems of counterbalance. Despite tightly knit organization, balance is never static and set. Oriented to what Picasso terms the "axis" of the picture, usually a strong diagonal pull, the elements are juxtaposed in such a way that they are continually in process of being equilibrated with the slight movement or oscillation at the moment of greatest suspense, when it is still not apparent whether the opposing elements will settle or whether the whole will topple over and crash.

As is the case with every other phase of these paintings, counterbalance is so complex as almost to defy analysis. Picasso nearly always uses highly unequal quantities of the same element and offsets this disparity by the distribution of other elements. The more apparent counterweight of a large form and small form with respectively quiet and active color takes place, as well as the less obvious one of the opposition of form to psychological content. If only a few of the opposites are considered: large-small, curved-angular, modeled-flat, object-idea, bright-dark, light-heavy, gay-sad, smooth-rough, realistic-abstract, and if one reflects on the interpenetration between different categories of these opposites, an idea may be had of the complexity with which the problem of balance is approached. Even the play between the third dimension, occasionally re-employed in recent canvases, and the two-dimensional concept itself (Plate 12) is ultimately a question of equilibrium. This equilibrium, then, is one that works laterally as well as away from and toward the observer.

The manner in which the active and live balance develops other *REVERSALS* ramifications may be seen in a highly interesting and important process of reversals. This is really philosophic in basis and informs his work in various degrees from a purely physical stage to one almost completely of idea.

In the plastic element of form, a physical stage, this is discernible in an interchangeable relationship between figure and ground (Gestalt form). Picasso defines by a common line adjacent foreground and background shapes. Through this device they both occupy the same plane, and, moreover, reverse their habitual order, thus alternating as figure and as ground (Plates 44, 115).

Carrying this a step further toward a purely ideational ultimate, in a still life before a landscape (not reproduced) Picasso referred to the still life as being on the second plane in deep space while the landscape, inversely, occupied the first plane.

Less tangible than reversal of form or of space is the reversal of idea. In *Reclining Nude and Woman Bathing* (Plate 11) the properties of a shadow are reversed, first by creating a highlight as it hits the pitcher upon the floor, and again when the pitcher is treated as a lamp that does not radiate light, but a shaft of darkness. This treatment of physical objects clearly expresses the acceptance of opposites by a complex personal dualism. Among other examples, *The Painter and His Model,* 1928, perhaps presents the same theme more succinctly. Here the painter, abstractly portrayed, working from a similarly abstract model, paints a naturalist profile of her.

The double image is another recurrent use of reversal. This is a type of metamorphosis which appears in still lifes, such as the recent pitcher-bird image (Plates 34, 117) or the above-mentioned pitcher-lamp; in others, objects are transformed by animation into personages (Plates 36, 118). All of these are double images, but because of their poetic nature, in Picasso's work they are closer to being what might be called painting metaphors, and these may be found there as early as cubism. In 1912 he made a *papier collé* titled *Head,* the contour of which also outlined the form of a guitar, while the ears of the head became the sound holes of the instrument. Throughout the years Picasso has introduced poetic changes of this kind, and in his recent work, when they make their appearance, they sometimes even form a continuity from one painting to another. Thus the pitcher becomes a lamp (Plate 11), the lamp a person (Plate 36), the person a vessel (Plate 10), completing a cycle of progressive, symbolic change.

More subtle is the reversal to be found in a progressive series of portraits. As these portraits become more abstract plastically, they inversely change from an abstract concept—the portrayal of the face as a mask and skull—to a more literal one which reverts to human features (Plates 88 to 93).

Because it merges several concepts, the double profile, increasingly prevalent in Picasso's work of recent years, is a fascinating development of his pictorial evolution. This is primarily another manifestation of the circulating viewpoint, but differs from his earlier portraits where the profile and full face were combined, forming a composite of two points of view. The presentation now is of three points of view: the two profiles and the full face, all of which are superimposed to form a single face. The right and left profile interlock in such a manner that, as the perception shifts, the image shifts from one to the other. The full face as well as the profiles all retain their original character, forming a double image wherein the face is equal to the sum of two profiles. Gestalt form and overlapping form engage in this visual game of shifting images (Plate 82).

By far the most impressive group of paintings made by Picasso during this period are his portraits and figure pieces. There are several phases of aesthetic variation involved in these portrayals, but many of them are characterized, as we have observed, by outraged feeling and distortion of the visual familiarity of animate objects far more disturbing than in landscape or still life.

P O R T R A I T S

Proceeding from the tortured quality of medieval Spanish religious paintings, which were so much a part of the *Guernica* series, Picasso, more subtly, has projected the violence of the war years, not in deliberate or obvious statements of Spanish blood and death, but through an emotional, sometimes symbolic, imagery which cuts deeply and lastingly into the most inaccessible levels of consciousness.

Still, despite their general character, these paintings portray people of many types and in many states of mind. For example, although one finds in the portraits as a whole enlarged nostrils, sensuous mouths or wild eyes, lascivious noses and twisted and deformed mouths, the facial expression may be basically gay, gentle, piquant, tranquil, religious, filled with wonder, amazement, pain, greed, cruelty, or madness. Just as the pictures contain all of the elements of representation, the manner in which these people appear on the canvas is that of formal portraiture. This is so in spite of the fierce originality of invention. Picasso's portraits are not of people posing, but of people remembered with the special, selective, and pitilessly penetrating clarity of this artist's memory.

Yet Picasso as a person is quite the opposite of what one might expect from these portrayals. Full of sparkling wit and fun, he is adored by children and adults, by the scores of casual acquaintances and tradespeople whom he encounters repeatedly in the streets and shops, and the hundreds of friends who are devoted to him. Only in his brittle dynamism, keen alertness, and piercing eye, can one observe in him the creator of these remarkable pictures.

There are also paintings more restrained through which he looks with sad dignity upon the sorrows of mankind. It is in these that the monotones prevail—grays, blacks, and browns; colors, if used, are psychologically morbid, such as the deep greens and sad purples previously mentioned. In Plates 82, 83, the slow-moving, continuous line makes a melancholy curvilinear pattern, while still another group of portraits in this mood are those which metamorphose into bitterly morose masks and sinister skulls (Plates 88, 89). Some of these pictures (Plates 50, 75, 90) show the face divided, one part smiling and animated, the other static and sad. These give the impression of a split personality, but are aesthetically so controlled that this very split or division presents a new idea of visual counterpoint.

STILL LIFE Seldom in the past did Picasso paint the abundant table; almost ascetic were the wine, tobacco, dessert, the newspaper, and musical instruments of his earlier periods, all reflecting relaxation and quiet enjoyment after the meal. Yet during the last five years he painted a number of still lifes with filled baskets, meat and fowl (Plates 25, 57), and this choice of subject may conceivably have been prompted by the concern over the food scarcity during the occupation. The deep interest with which the tomato plant was painted in 1944 may also be indicative of this concern.

The many versions of this plant which grew on his studio window sill and bore edible fruit were done with such affection and charm that they remain a symbol of care and tenderness.

On the other hand, the depleted *Buffet Chez Catalan* (Plate 60), and, above all, the many still lifes of animal and human skulls containing also withered leeks, empty pitchers, and dim lamplight, are poignant with the feeling of hunger and poverty and of death (Plates 64, 117).

In yet another group (Plates 32, 35, 36) there is a playful animation of the objects, which are converted through poetic metamorphosis into personages of high fantasy. Arranged on a table, they become actors on a stage. All of the objects animated are just sufficiently out of equilibrium to suggest movement, and give the feeling that some magnetic force operating beneath the table manipulates them. In Plate 35 the little drama consists of the intercession of a nunlike candlestick between a belligerent hourglass pitcher and a timid casserole. Plate 36 features a lamp which is a combination of a pompous dowager and the cartoon character Popeye swinging into action. The French sailor coffeepot in Plate 33 addresses a prismatic "mirror, mirror on the wall" and in another painting of the same date (Plate 37) the magic mirror shows him "who is the fairest of them all."

The mirror, traditionally associated with magic, is recurrently used in the figure and still-life pictures, not as the customary narcissist mechanism, but as a symbol of inner vision, which Picasso otherwise visualizes in terms of light (Plates 6, 8, 10, 33).

FANTASY AND MAGIC

The fantasy of play and magic, as well as the myth and mystery of Picasso's totemic portraiture, the ecstasy of dream, the shock of surprise, all invoke the surrealist image. The surrealists found much of their point of view latent in the techniques and achievements of *collage*. Anticipating their first manifesto by a dozen years, these developed through Dada to eventually crystallize as one of the facets of surrealist ideology. Though Picasso was never a member of this group, no exhibit is arranged or book published by them without a representation from some phase of his work. The underlying identifiable realism and superstructure of imagery and symbolic meaning in his paintings establish a spontaneous surreality over which the surrealists themselves show the greatest enthusiasm.

PARIS SCENES

In the past forty years Picasso has done comparatively few landscape subjects. The group of some twenty Paris scenes made during the war equals perhaps his total previous output. These Seine scenes, a particularly well-integrated series, painted in a new interpretation of 1909 facet cubism, are tightly interlocked by a powerful linear construction which is the predominating motif in each painting. Reflecting Parisian overcast days, they are low in color key, some in black and gray monotones, others in lavenders and deep purples (Plates 43, 113). Still others, painted on the fourteenth of July, were less somber in color as a restrained tribute to the spirit of the day (Plate 116). Quite different are the scenes done in 1940, such as *The Café, Royan* (Plate 15), which is gayer, more decorative, even somewhat carnival in spirit. The horrors of war, of the cold and hungry years ahead, were not yet apparent in his work. Still in the same year, in early June, as if with an uncanny prescience, Picasso painted several skull-like heads in the green-tan color of the German uniforms. On the eve of the fall of Paris he was perhaps already painting the death of Germany.

COMPARISONS— THE WAR PERIODS

The difference between the work of Picasso in World War I and in World War II is striking. The start of the earlier war found him on the threshold of synthetic cubism. Already behind him were facet and analytical cubism and *collage*. Further back was the Negroid Period (1906–8) in which his maturity as an artist had begun to take definite form. In 1916–17 his easel work became, for him, quite decorative. Accomplishing comparatively little in a creative way during this short time, he regained his adventurous spirit when, near the close of the first war, he began to paint the first of his "Colossal" Period pictures. Before this, in 1917, Picasso had gone to Italy to do costumes and scenery for the Ballet Russe. It was there he married the dancer, Olga Koklova, of whom he had painted several fine portraits in the classic manner. This classic style which he had originally adopted in 1905 he reverted to in 1915, after the innovations of cubism.

The World War II period, as pointed out, was a highly productive and wrathful one. Much of it was a continuation of work done in the second half of the thirties. However, the latter, in spite of physiognomical displacements and anti-naturalism, had gaiety and humor, with the exception of the *Guernica*. If this painting and its many studies were the recording at white heat of an outburst of titanic anger, they were at the same time full of the deepest compassion and humanity. By the forties this anger had turned almost fatalistically sardonic.

That primitivism as the initial or archaic phase of a cultural cycle is the dominant tendency of our time is a conclusion deriving equally from scientific and artistic premises. The archaic tenor of this period, arising from a new era introduced by the discovery and invention of new techniques for living, exists with categorical parallel in the work of Picasso. It was Picasso who, more than any other living artist, found in the archaic or primitive spirit its best and truest meaning. Primitive art derives its means of communication from its invention and use of symbols, and its power from the primitive way of looking at reality. To the primitive mind all things, seen or unseen, are equally real. There is no line of demarcation between the natural and supernatural, for all things conceivable are natural. Magic is thus an accredited part of life, and it is this magic, almost lost to human beings, that Picasso's painting, oriented to our day, restores to us.

Because their civilizations appear so different from ours, the art of primitive peoples and the salutary integrity of the primitive viewpoint are often misunderstood. Their cultures, perhaps narrower than ours, are frequently more basic and more profound.

Primitive cultures of Oceania, Africa, pre-Inca America, and other parts of the world accept, as the norm of tribal tradition, abstract

PICASSO AND ARCHAIC ART

imagery with its inevitable distortion and its transposition of elements of the human form into magic masks and fetishes.

In the comparatively small units of tribal societies, the masks provide a homogeneous aesthetic for all. Conceived in relation to primitive lore, they play a special role in social and religious functions. As a result, the members are conditioned or accustomed to live with the abstract imagery of their magic.

In our age of specialization the aesthetic outlook is divided into many schisms, each of which has its own adherents. Furthermore, the general techniques of the visual arts are not only many, but highly complex. For example, there is painting in many varieties, *collage*, sculpture, object-making, photography, and the motion picture, each with its own intrinsic aesthetic. Today the individual must reconcile these different contemporary creative sources before he can possess a homogeneous aesthetic vision, one comparable in its wholeness to the primitive point of view.

Technological masks such as the gas, ether, and welder's mask exist in great quantity in our civilization, as well as the social masks used in sports (baseball catcher's mask) and in carnivals and masquerades. The camouflage used in war is, in a wider sense, a mask. Our protective coloration and the primitive's garish array to frighten the enemy are opposite techniques aimed at the same objective. The camouflage of World War I was already anticipated in the field of aesthetics, for it was literally a stylization of the flat areas and space divisions of *collage* (1912–13). These, in turn, were an extension of the basic character of cubism in which the individual identities of objects in a picture were subordinated as the objects and background merged on a single plane to form a new unification.

While the technological and sports masks have a utility and the carnival masks varying degrees of psychological and emotional value, none has the incantational power the magic masks of the primitive are known to have for him.

With the most comprehensive understanding of the aesthetic parallels to our scientific age and modern life, Picasso accomplishes in his work what the primitives achieve in their ceremonial masks and fetishes. Though the mask is so prominent in the war-period portraits, it has appeared repeatedly, either directly or by inference, throughout his work since the profound impact of African sculpture, in 1906, upon his sensitive and intuitive mind. Selecting and utilizing physical and psychological characteristics peculiar to the mask, he has converted them into magic images of his own making. Like the primitives, Picasso creates imagery equal in power and in poetic relation to the spirit and character of his own culture. He establishes thereby similar conditions for intense emotional experience and for a true feeling of identification and communication, not with the external supernatural as they do, but with those forces which correspond, in reality, to the primitive super-natural—the natural creative forces in man.

PLATES

AND COMMENTARY

In the foreground is Picasso's palette—a packing case covered with newspaper—upon which he mixes colors out of cans (Ripolin) as well as out of tubes of pigment. Ripolin, which gives a smooth finish, was unobtainable during the war. Picasso had a large supply on hand, and stretched it by mixing it with tube paint. When it eventually ran out, he painted with tube paint alone.

The canvases photographed above, many of which are now privately owned in France, are stacked against the reverse side of a large picture—the unfinished *The Charnel House*. Behind this, against the back wall, is a door panel sent by an art patron who had asked Picasso to paint on it, as a commission, a picture for her home. Today, years later, the panel still remains untouched.

PLATE 3

View of the Hanging of Picasso Paintings at the Salon d'Automne, 1944.

PLATE 4

As above, the hanging on the opposite wall. In the lower photograph the camera angle aligns the sculpture *Coq* on the pedestal with the painting of the same subject on the wall, creating the amusing illusion that the sculpture stepped out of the canvas. Another version of *Coq* is reproduced in Plate 111.

PLATE 5

Night Fishing at Antibes, *Royan, August 1939. Oil on Canvas, 84 x 136"*.

This is Picasso's largest picture since *Guernica*. Painted just before the start of the war, it portrays two night fishermen, both leaning over the side of a small boat, spearing fish under artificial light. To the right, two figures on the pier watch the activity. One portrays Dora Maar holding a bicycle with one hand, and in the other a double-scoop ice-cream cone which she is eating. The other figure, Jacqueline Breton-Lamba, stands by idly.

Picasso made a large series of sketches and paintings based on the theme of two women, of which seven versions are reproduced in the following group. A reclining nude occupies the central position in each. In this early version the standing figure is placed behind the couch and holds a striped cloth which she is about to spread. The coverlet is twisted by this movement into an hourglass shape, at the center of which the color stripes converge.

A mirrored wardrobe door, half open, is seen at the foot of the couch. The mirror plays a prominent role, either mysterious, magical, or metaphysical, in several paintings of this series.

Here it possesses simultaneously the qualities of reflection and transparency, for upon its surface are reflected light patterns while through it can be seen the feet of the recumbent figure.

The mirror is, in effect, a framed picture of a pair of feet. Below, a series of legs: of the attendant, the couch, and the wardrobe, seem to parade across the base of the canvas.

The couch seen at the same time from above and below and the bodies as well as the faces of the nudes, also seen from simultaneous viewpoints, are aspects of Picasso's device of the circulating viewpoint. (Plates 8, 11, 96. Pages 28, 29).

Color heightens the structural tensions within the picture which integrate the figures and the various objects. Color inventively introduced as modeling on the reclining nude here becomes the initial focal point.

COLOR PLATE 6

Reclining and Standing Nudes, *Paris, February 1, 1942. Oil on Paper, 12 x 16",*.

PLATE 7

Sketch for Woman With Mandolin and Reclining Nude, *Paris, May 3, 1942.*
Ink on Paper, 10 x 6¾".

Here the reclining nude and the mandolinist have not yet assumed the
ultimate position they are to occupy in the large oil (Plate 8). In this sketch,
tonal emphasis is achieved by highlighting the beam of the lamp under
which the nude basks (center), as well as the rectangular area within the
frame of the opened wardrobe mirror door (left).

PLATE 8

Woman with Mandolin, and Reclining Nude (formerly, Odalisque), *Paris, May 1942. Oil on Canvas, 76 x 103".*

The largest and most important of the series of two women. The nude reclines on a striped divan, arms behind her head, while the other figure is seated, hand in lap, holding a mandolin. On the floor at the left is the mirror found in so many paintings of this period, setting the theme for the dynamic lines which operate as reflected and refracted tensions of light throughout the entire picture. These expand dramatically, and constitute a highly integrated structure within the painting.

PLATE 8

PLATE 9

Reclining Nude, *Paris, April 21, 1944. Oil on Canvas, 15 x 18".*

In this version of the two women theme, the secondary figure is represented to the right as a configuration upon a canvas—a painting within a painting—the edges of which are shown tacked on the stretcher. The mirror is now full face to the observer, and its reflected light radiates in the direction of the standing canvas. Despite this strong spotlighting, the picture in the background remains in the shadow. This is another variation on the idea of reversal (Pages 31, 32).

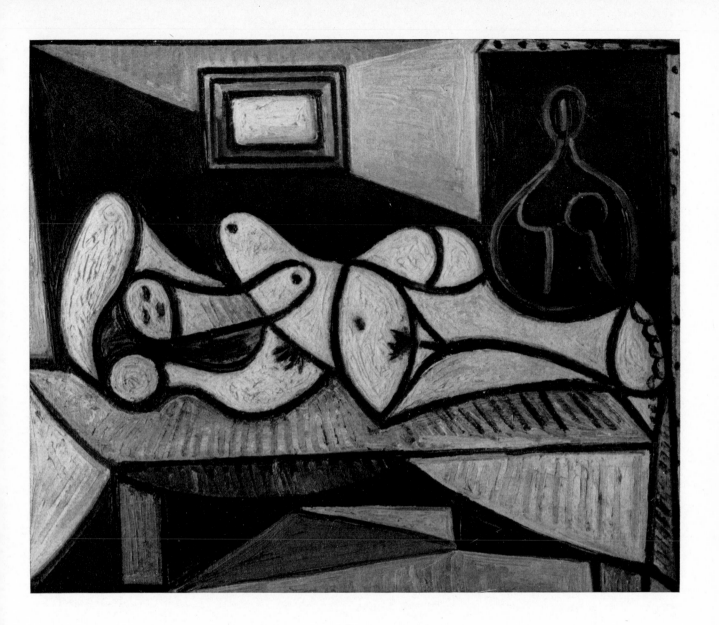

PLATE 9

PLATE 10

Interior, Seated Woman and Standing Nude, *Paris, April 1944. Oil on Canvas, 28 x 36".*

Light enters the room from the window (behind the nude) in many directions and at various degrees of intensity. In the rapport established between the window and the mirror on the wardrobe door (left), a reversal in direction of light takes place. Now heightened and reflected, it cuts across the seated figure to converge at the windowpane. Thus, not only does this beam of light move in a direction opposite to daylight, but its physical properties are also reversed. The light no longer radiates but converges, as if the mirror were a magic eye focusing on a point at the window.

Compare standing figure with Plates 121, 123, painted in 1946.

PLATE 10

PLATE 11

Reclining Nude and Woman Bathing Her Feet, *Paris, August 18, 1944. Oil on Canvas, 38 x 51".*

Here the magic mirror is replaced by a kind of magic lantern, really a water pitcher on the floor. A shaft, not of light, but of shadow, emerges from it, centering upon the figure bathing. Broken by the couch, it resumes in the upper right corner.

The figure on the couch offers an opportunity to observe clearly and simply the pictorial device of the circulating viewpoint, or simultaneity, the delineation of several sides of a given object at the same time. Here the front and rear views of the figure are shown side by side. Picasso first used this device in a *Standing Nude* of the late Negroid Period in 1908. Variations of simultaneous seeing, which appear repeatedly throughout Picasso's career, may be observed in several of the two women series, as well as in many of the recent portraits and still lifes (Plates 13, 62).

PLATE 11

PLATE 12

Reclining Nude, *Paris, September 30, 1942. Oil on Canvas, 51 x 77"*.

In depicting this powerful nude, a woman reclining on a mat, Picasso carried the circulating *viewpoint* into further detail. Because so much of the back is shown, the figure is necessarily turned away from the observer, yet equal detail is given to the front view.

The treatment of this figure is similar to that of the musical instrument in cubism and *collage*, where opposite sides were presented on the same picture plane.

The introduction in the picture reproduced here of extensive modeling, omitted in cubism, tends to destroy the cubist two-dimensional premise. The mat, however, ensnaring the figure with its linear meshlike arrangement, remains on a single plane. While this counteracts the suggestion created by modeling, the whole takes on the appearance of a relief plaque.

Two Women: Nude Standing and Woman Seated, *Royan, September 23, 1939, Oil on Panel, 16 x 13"*.

Here again the simultaneous views of the front and back of the standing figure are given. Moreover, the circulating viewpoint, brought to the configuration of the face, logically explains the appearance of eyes and nostrils all on the same profile. Opening up like the covers of a book, both sides of the face appear on the same plane. However disquieting these anatomical juxtapositions may be to the observer, Picasso is able to attain thereby a deeply penetrating psychological characterization.

The inverted V-shaped supports of the chair, emulating the legs of the figures, become bipeds which join the others in casual repose along the base of the picture.

PLATE 13

PLATE 15

The Café, Royan, *August 15, 1940. Oil on Canvas, 38 x 51".*

Picasso's Royan studio, shown in the center of the canvas, was bombed out of existence by the Allied Air Force shortly before the liberation.

PLATE 16

The Charnel House, *Paris, 1944—   . Oil on Canvas, 78 x 97½".*

Begun in 1944, this picture has been worked on intermittently since, but is still unfinished. It was exhibited in the above state at the Art and Resistance Exhibition, Paris, February 1946.

Painted in cold colors of steel gray, black and white, it depicts the corpses of a man, woman, and child. The starved and tortured man lies face down across the composition, his arms propped and tied behind him, his feet extending beyond the legs of the table. The woman, face up, her head resting on the legs of the man, lies in the opposite direction, her feet at the lower right. The child is also on its back, its feet pointing at right angles to the mother. On a table to the rear are a pitcher, a casserole, and a disheveled tablecloth. Toward the upper right, in unfinished state, swirling lines sweep upward. These and the flicker of light which becomes more agitated as it approaches the right side of the picture suggest flame. *The Charnel House* pictures humanity as if immolated on a funeral pyre.

PLATE 17

Picasso in his Studio at Royan with Jaime Sabartés, his secretary and closest friend. Canvas on Easel: *Seated Nude Combing Her Hair,* 1940.

PLATE 18

Throughout a friendship of almost fifty years Picasso has done many portraits of Sabartés, two of the earliest dating from 1901. Picasso here depicts his friend in the garb of a seventeenth-century scholar. The portrait remains readily recognizable despite the extreme displacement of the features.

PLATE 18

Portrait of Jaime Sabartés, *Royan, October 22, 1939. Oil on Canvas, 18 x 15".*

PLATE 19

All of the twenty-five canvases included in this show except one, the largest, *Night Fishing at Antibes* (hung below the Picasso placard and privately owned), are the property of the artist. The exhibition subsequently traveled to Glasgow, Birmingham, Brussels, and Amsterdam, causing lively controversy wherever shown (Page 17).

PLATES 19 AND 20

Two walls of Picasso paintings in the Picasso-Matisse Exhibition at the Victoria and Albert Museum, London, December 1945.

PLATE 20

PLATE 21

The Studio Window, *Paris, July 3, 1943. Oil on Canvas, 51 x 38″.*

PLATE 22

View from Picasso's Studio Window

In comparing the actual photograph with that of the painting opposite, the radiator valve (below the window sill) may serve as a point of orientation. While Picasso takes great liberties in transcribing this scene, it remains literal even to the point of including the hanging cloth to the left. The rearrangement of the view through the window has been quite extensive. In the photograph the side of the tallest building forms a huge J as it curves along the roofs below. In the painting this is modified radically, for it becomes a shortened arc pictorially tying in the roof and the window frame. This J configuration is punctuated below by a small square window, neutrally gray in the photograph but strongly accentuated in the painting. This and the radiator valve are two compelling focal points in the picture, whereas in the photograph they are just two of many details of equal value.

Beyond the various structural lines of tension which Picasso has introduced pictorially, the most radical change is the elimination of the furthermost building and its chimneys, one of which, in the photograph, stands out above the others against the sky. In the painting Picasso has brought the sky down to the next building, where the photograph shows the four squat chimneys. These are included in the painting, although one is seen through the french window at the left.

Across the top of the photograph the stone ledge over the window forms a broken-edged silhouette while in the painting this jagged contour, though simplified, cuts its way across the sky.

The camera, with its fixed focus, was unable to include the three smoke-stacks on the right and also the window below them; it failed to register the multi-facets and multi-tensions recorded through the sensibility of Picasso's vision.

PLATES 23 AND 24

Two Views of the Picasso Exhibition at Galerie Louis Carré, Paris, June 1945.

PLATE 25

Still Life, Basket of Fruit with Pitcher of Spice, *Paris, August 1942. Oil on Canvas, 28 x 36".*

PLATE 27

Still Life, Basket of Fruit and Pitcher with Spice, *Paris,*
August 13, 1943. Oil on Canvas, 28 x 36".

canvas where the pitcher of spice is almost simplified
out of existence. In the final version, while the basket of
fruit still remains, only a crystallization of the spice is
visible. The pictures reproduced here are painted from
three successive points of view, the first slightly below
eye level, the second lower, and the third lowest, seen
directly from above.

PLATE 26

Still Life, Basket of Fruit and Pitcher with Spice, *Paris,*
1942. Oil on Canvas, 32 x 39".

Of the several canvases in this arrangement, Plate 25
is the most realistic and perhaps the most powerful.
As this theme was reiterated, the subject became progressively more abstract, the latest (Plate 27), being
simplified to an almost completely rectilinear design.
Indicating briefly this evolution, the half-concealed
mirror of the first example disappears in the middle

PLATE 28

Tomato Plant at the Window, *Paris, August 10, 1944. Oil on Canvas, 36 x 28"*.

PLATE 29

Tomato Plant before the Window, *Paris, August 6, 1944. Oil on Canvas, 36 x 28".*

Tomato Plant, *Paris, August 4, 1944. Oil on Canvas, 28 x 36″.*

The preceding plate (29) is the most realistic version of the series of the tomato plant. Still, the configuration of the flowerpot and saucer there is almost completely abstract. The pot seems to be transparent, permitting a view of darkened segments of both saucer and windowpane which are behind it.

PLATE 31

Tomato Plant and Decanter, *Paris, August 3, 1944. Oil on Canvas, 28 x 36".*

PLATE 32

Still Life, *Paris, April 6, 1944. Oil on Canvas, 36 x 25".*

Picasso arranged in several canvases the identical sub-ject of a candlestick, coffeepot, apple, cup and saucer, and drinking glass upon a table before a mirror. The objects are given a kind of animation; they play "follow the leader." Still, in each picture the movement intro-duced works differently, and each composition remains unique. Here the objects form a train along the edge of the table, one affectionately attached to the next. The mirror also joins, playing caboose to the candleholder, which leads the procession.

The object next to the drinking glass, identified as the cup and saucer, and alongside of it an apple, make a configuration of a bowl of fruit, the base of which is actually the saucer. The half-round ellipse of the saucer along the side of the cup resembles a piece of fruit. The round form next to it, which is the top of the cup, re-sembles a second fruit, the cup handle a third, the darker round form of the apple next to it still another. The composite impression of fruit piled on a dish gives one the feeling that Picasso, surfeited perhaps with ersatz coffee, unconsciously substituted for the cup and saucer the wishful image of a more satisfying dish.

PLATE 33

Still Life with Mirror, *Paris, July 9, 1945. Oil on Canvas,*

35 x 45½".

The paraphernalia of this still life plainly consist of a lamp, cup and saucer, coffeepot, and a bowl of cherries on the table before a mirror. The canvas is divided, blacks, whites, and grays falling to one side, and bright color in smaller areas to the other. The mirror reflects upon its surface an array of prismatic color, and the cherries in the dish seem to swim in the kaleido-scope of reds and greens reflected by the mirror.

Color assists form in setting up a precarious pictorial balance, for the blacks, whites, and grays establish within their own range a series of contrasts which counterbalance those obtained within the bright color areas. The light background effectively heightens this dramatic action.

The still life in this plate forms a procession across the canvas similar to the animated still life in Plate 32. The various objects, a bird perched on a stand, flowers in the pitcher, sculptured head on the table, and the hanging mirror, do not touch each other as do those in the other canvas, but are just as inextricably connected by the facets of light and shade which link them firmly together as by a chain. These facets, cutting across both figure and ground, forge the links and unite both objects and space between objects. In contradistinction to the accents of light and dark, the introduction of pastel color holds the picture in a subtle balance of interest. The focal point is the mirror where yellow, the brightest color in the painting, bursts like sunbeams along the mirror frame.

A bird motif is reflected in nearby objects. Facing the bird stand, the pitcher assumes the form of a bird, while the sculptured head, with its birdlike features, calls to mind Brancusi's sculpture, *Bird in Space.*

COLOR PLATE 34

Still Life with Mirror, *Paris, June 7, 1945. Oil on Canvas, 32 x 45½".*

PLATE 36

Still Life with Lamp, *Paris, July 9, 1945. Oil on Canvas, 28 x 39".*

The propensity of an object to undergo transformation is often encountered in Picasso's work. Everyday objects metamorphose into new images, magical, humorous, or poetic. A pitcher takes on the guise of a bird (Plate 34) or, as in this still life, a lamp becomes a personage—a standing figure of a woman with widely extended elbows. She wears a peach-basket hat and around her neck a fluted collar. The projecting lever (the wick control) cannot be accounted for unless it is the key with which to wind the toylike personage. A further note of the fantasy and metamorphic play in this as well as other figures appears on page 35.

PLATE 37

Still Life with Mirror Reflection, *Paris, July 9, 1945. Oil on Canvas,* 25½ x 39".

The introduction of the face in the mirror, although it is only a reflection, carries with it an element of the unexpected, even of the supernatural, endowing the painting with surrealist overtones. The drinking glass poised at the very edge of the table adds to the element of surprise.

This still life, characterized by a delightful animation, is the third of the same subject painted the same day.

PLATE 38

Pont St. Michel.

PLATE 39

Notre Dame Cathedral from Pont St. Michel.

PLATE 40

Notre Dame Cathedral from Pont St. Michel.

PLATE 41

Picasso's Studio, March 1946.

This group of smaller oils of Paris scenes was casually arranged against the easel by Picasso himself during a conversation. To the right is the newspaper-covered stand which serves as his palette.

PLATE 42

PLATE 42

View of Notre Dame Cathedral, *Paris, May 21, 1944. Oil on Canvas, 13 x 7½″.*

This is the most representational canvas of the series of Paris scenes. The extent to which Picasso has nevertheless rearranged the actual aspects may be judged from the fact that three photographs (Plates 38, 39, 40) were necessary to record the points of view he has compressed into one painting. Picasso has elongated the arch of Pont St. Michel in order to enclose the façade of Notre Dame, whereas in the photograph (Plate 40), though the camera places the cathedral in a similar position, the arch of the bridge is more nearly horizontal. This view could only be obtained from under the bridge, in which position neither the façade nor the balustrade could be included. In order to present a view of both the façade of the bridge and the cathedral, the photograph reproduced in Plate 39 was taken, but here the various buildings are visible above and not below the bridge, as in the painting. The third photograph (Plate 38) shows the balustrade of the bridge against the sky and the boats in the Seine below, as they are in the painting, but La Cité is no longer in view.

The wreath which marks the bridge is in a corresponding position in the painting. Picasso pointed out this detail in the upper left-hand corner of the canvas, saying: "Here is the space for the 'N' for Napoleon."

Under the high arch to the extreme right in the painting appears the steeple, cut off at the top by the arch. But photographing the steeple in this relation to the cathedral towers would necessitate moving the camera a block nearer the church, well beyond the bridge. In fact, if all the details of which this painting is a composite were to be recorded accurately, it would be necessary to take photographs from many other positions as well.

The paintings of the Paris scenes that follow are variations of this setting, and afford an opportunity to compare the more abstract scenes with this painting and with the photographs of the actual scene.

PLATE 43

Paris, la Cité, *February 26, 1945. Oil on Canvas,*

32 x 39".

This view of Notre Dame, the surrounding buildings, and the nearby bridges is perhaps Picasso's most important canvas in this series. Although it is impossible to see Montmartre from this approach to Notre Dame, Picasso has pictorially introduced, at the highest point in the canvas, the domes of Sacré Cœur (left).

Perspective is implied by the fact that the bridge in the foreground is large, the Notre Dame in the middle smaller, and the forms of the Sacré Cœur in the background smallest. The pictorial construction of this Paris view, however, resembles a highly developed stage of facet cubism, in which these points, no longer in deep space, are now presented two-dimensionally. Thus foreground and background are given equal value. In fact, they even reverse their respective positions in a visual play of oscillating planes. This interchange of figure and ground is even more pronounced in Plate 115.

Lines of tension, like beams of light, radiate from the steeple of Notre Dame (center) and, projecting to the left, connect with the domes of the Sacré Cœur. This is a clear example of the manner in which the lines of prismatic light become part of the structure of the picture.

PLATE 45

Head of a Woman, *Royan, May 24, 1940. Oil on Board, 17 x 5¾″.*

PLATE 46

Head of a Woman, *Royan, August 22, 1940. Oil on Board, 14 x 4¾″.*

Both of these paintings, reminiscent of the painting on New Guinea shields, were done on the wooden boards of a packing case.

PLATE 47

Photograph of Miss Dora Maar at her Worktable, Paris, March 1946.

On the easel is a painting recently finished. A Picasso portrait of Miss Maar (1944) hangs above the fireplace. The six plates that follow, all Portraits of D. M., move progressively toward abstraction. However, although they range from comparative literalism to abstract morphology, they were not painted in this order.

PLATE 48

Portrait of D. M., *Paris, April 20, 1941. Oil on Canvas, 28 x 23".*

PLATE 49

Portrait of D. M., *Paris, May 29, 1941. Oil on Canvas, 21½ x 18″.*

Portrait of D. M., *Paris, October 9, 1942. Oil on Canvas, 36 x 28".*

The psychological aspect of this portrait is of great interest. By dividing the background into two contrasting areas, Picasso establishes the theme of divisionism, dark versus light. While this theme is self-evident in the background, it next appears more subtly and inventively in the face. Here the opposing qualities of surface and depth, the inner and the outer, are suggested by nuance, and become manifest in the portrait as dual aspects of her personality. Corresponding to the dark side of the background, the features on the right half of the face, reflecting the mood, are tense, characterized by dilated nostril, penetrating eye, firm jaw, sharp upper lip, set mouth. On the lighter side, however, the features register the outer mood in softer, smoother, more placid contours.

Color also plays a psychological part. Applied to the features in a minute mosaic of red, green, and tan, the color appears more agitated to the right. The aggregate of these contrasts in expression accentuates all the more the cleavage between the two sides of the personality. The drawing of the shoulders is also consistent with the theme of divisionism, the left side being expansive and the right depressed. While it may have been compositionally feasible to place the figure off center, this also is symbolic, for her position in front of the lighter ground conveys the idea that she prefers to be known in her lighter mood. Yet, since there is some overlapping of the figure against the shadow, the inference is that despite outer calm the inner turbulence of the sitter comes through.

Picasso's great mastery of pigment and color is revealed in the lustrous surface and luscious color of the striped silk dress.

This *Portrait of D. M.*, painted over a period of weeks, was started shortly before the death of her mother. As the patient grew worse, D. M. became more and more distressed. Simultaneously the picture, too, underwent changes, evidence of which may be seen in the underpainting.

PLATE 51

Portrait of D. M., *Paris, September 20, 1942. Oil on Canvas, 28 x 23".*

PLATE 52

Portrait of D. M., *Paris, April 26, 1942. Oil on Canvas, 18 x 15".*

This painting, hung in a darkened room in Miss Maar's apartment, created a remarkable effect of luminosity. Its white areas vibrated nervously in contrast with the surrounding darks.

PLATE 53

Portrait of D. M., *Royan, April 1, 1939. Oil on Canvas, 36 x 28″*.

It was only after Miss Maar had seen this picture again and again that she noticed a small bulb-ous contour on her own forehead similar to that shown with strong exaggeration here.

PLATE 54

A wall of the "Picasso room" in the home of Mme. Cuttoli, Paris. Paintings reproduced above date from 1937 to 1945. The large farmyard scene (center), a pastel on canvas, has never been exhibited or reproduced before. Upon seeing it in March 1946 for the first time since it left his hands before the war, Picasso admiringly remarked: "Not bad!"

Woman Feeding a Cat (second canvas from right) was reproduced in color in 1945 by the French Government as an experiment, with an almost perfect result.

PLATE 55

Corner of Galerie Louise Leiris (Kahnweiler), Paris, showing the recent Picasso paintings in its collection.

PLATE 56

Still Life, Paris, December 2, 1943. Oil on Canvas, 15 x 21½".

PLATE 57

Still Life with Dead Fowl, *Paris 1942. Oil on Canvas, 23½ x 28".*

PLATE 58

View of Le Vert-Galant, Paris, March 1946.

A comparison of the photograph above and the painting opposite will throw considerable light on the realism in Picasso's work. Although the oil is studio-made and not *plein-air,* Picasso has retained all of the essential details in their original setting. In both photograph and painting the old Canadian poplar trees form a huge N; the two doorways appear beneath the arch of the trees; the kiosk is at the right; and cutting horizontally across the center in each is the balustrade of the bridge (*Pont Neuf*).

Le Vert-Galant is a little park at the tip of the Isle de la Cité, not far from

PLATE 59

Le Vert-Galant, *Paris, June 25, 1943. Oil on Canvas, 25½ x 36″.*

Picasso's studio. It is the rendezvous for lovers that inspired the *Kissers* series (Plate 112), the idea for which will be incorporated in a large oil also to be titled *Le Vert-Galant* (page 5). The park was named for Henry IV, whose equestrian statue can be seen against the sky. In the painting the statue is seen in profile, but the angle necessary for the camera to record this viewpoint would have excluded the park. The painting was done in June, which accounts for the abundant foliage; the photograph was taken in March.

Still Life with Blut-Wurst, *Paris, May 10, 1941. Oil on Canvas, 35 x 25½".*

This still life, a serving table at Le Savoyard is mournfully pervaded by tones of gray, black, and white, its only colors. In the words of Picasso, it has "an atmosphere like Philip II, dark and dismal." Describing it further, Picasso observed: "The knives and forks are like souls out of Purgatory."

PLATE 60

PLATE 61

Buffet Chez Catalan, *Paris, May 30, 1943. Oil on Canvas, 32 x 39″*.

In an introduction to *Picasso-Seize Peintures, 1939–43*, Robert Desnos recounts a reference to this still life as told by Picasso: "I have been dining at Chez Catalan for many months, and for many months I have been seeing their buffet not thinking it anything other than a buffet. One day I decided to make a picture of it. I made it. The day before yesterday when I arrived, the buffet was not to be seen. Its place was vacant. . . . I took it, without my knowing, in painting it."

PLATE 61

PLATE 62

Still Life on the Table, *Paris, October 25, 1941. Oil on Canvas, 32 x 39".*

PLATE 63

Still Life with Skull and Leeks, *Paris, 1945. Oil on Canvas, 38 x 51".*

A brief identification of objects is given on page 25. Other paintings of the same subject, Plates 64 and 65, are but two of several in this series.

PLATE 64

Still Life with Skull and Leeks, *Paris, March 13, 1945. Oil on Canvas, 32 x 45½".*

PLATE 65

Still Life with Skull and Leeks, Paris, March 14, 1945. Oil on Canvas, 28 x 45½".

PLATE 66

Still Life Against White Background, *Paris, August 6, 1943. Oil on Canvas, 21 x 32".*

The most striking passage in this still life is the configuration of the three drinking glasses. Beyond the mournful appearance caused by the myriad lines which curve through them there is also a suggestion within each of sleeping seated figures with heads bowed resting on encircled arms. These figures recall the three sleepers in the cave of El Greco's *Christ on the Mount of Olives,* National Gallery, London. Here each sleeper occupies his own cave.

PLATE 67

Woman in a Rocking Chair, *Paris, August 9, 1943. Oil on Canvas, 64 x 51".*

"The floor rears up like a wave behind the rocking chair"—ERIC NEWTON, *Picture Post, London, Dec. 22, 1945.*

PLATE 68

Vase of Gladioli on a Chair, *Paris, September 17, 1943. Oil on Canvas, 57½ x 45″.*

PLATE 69

Child and Pigeons, *Paris, August 24, 1943. Oil on Canvas, 64 x 51".*

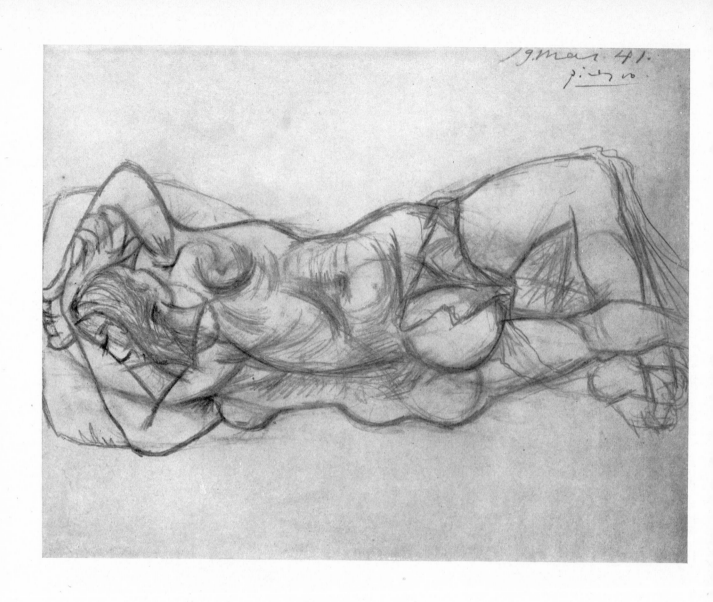

PLATE 70

Study, Reclining Nude, *Paris, May 19, 1941. Pencil on Paper.*

PLATE 73

Head of a Woman, *Paris, May 25, 1941. Oil on Canvas, 16 x 13".*

PLATE 72

Seated Woman, *Paris, July 26, 1941. Oil on Canvas, 36 x 28".*

PLATE 71

Seated Woman with Cat, *Paris, 1944. Oil on Canvas.*

PLATES 71–77

Picasso's portraits and figures are of cardinal importance. They are his most vital paintings of the war years. Distorted, grotesque, anguished, convulsed, pensive, or gay, they offend, sting, challenge, or shock the observer. The creative artist necessarily being in advance of his audience, his work is often baffling at first sight.

In the following groups of portraits, though pictorial ideas overlap, the canvases fall into markedly separate categories. It must be emphasized that at no time did Picasso paint any of these pictures as a series. On the contrary, since they do not follow a chronological order, the paintings disclose the fact that he reverts continually to a given pictorial theme, projecting the ever-changing images of a many-faceted vision (pages 25, 34).

It has been observed that Picasso never works directly from the model. His portraits are of persons remembered. They portray, through the instinct and vision, through the delicately balanced co-ordination of eye, mind, hand, and heart, a new realism reaching into the deepest recesses of man's inner nature. This is particularly true of the first group (Plates 71 to 77), for all of these portrayals, psychologically intense and penetrating, become increasingly so throughout the group. Characterized by the extreme eccentricity and psychopathic distortion of their personalities, the likenesses are visibly stamped with their traumatic scars.

PLATE 74

Woman in Wicker Chair, *Paris, May 27, 1941. Oil on Canvas, 28 x 23½″.*

Seated Woman before a Figured Background, *Paris, October 1941*.

PLATE 76

Woman with Flowered Hat, *Royan, October 11, 1939, May 5, 1940. Oil on Canvas, 28 x 23½".*

PLATE 77

Woman with Bouquet, *Paris, 1942. Oil on Canvas, 77 x 51″.*

PLATE 78

The wicker chair in Picasso's studio, used in the painting opposite, may also be seen in Plate 74.

PLATES 79–84

The following group of curvilinear portraits, primarily in monotones, has an over-all character of wistfulness in contrast to the bright countenance of the portrait in Color Plate 81, also in the series. Present in all of the pictures is a dramatic lighting similar to that in the color reproduction. The degree to which its intensity eats away form accounts for the partially reduced physiognomy which appears in the final picture (Plate 84).

PLATE 79

Head of a Woman, *Paris, May 17–July 9, 1943. Oil on Canvas, 25½ x 21".*

PLATE 80

Woman Holding an Apple, *Paris, March 7, 1944. Oil on Canvas, 36 x 23½″.*

COLOR PLATE 81

Figure Seated in Wicker Chair, *Paris, September 24, 1943. Oil on Canvas, 39 x 32"*.

As in all the work of Picasso, habitual visual responses to physical appearance are here subordinated to a more inventive morphology. In this picture, light and color are, above other plastic elements, the most active and influential. Although color obviously is of great importance, it is dependent upon the accentuations of light for its high-pitched or muted effects. Line and form are even more under the domination of light, the quantity and intensity of which dictate and control the ultimate shapes and patterns. Light and shade model and carve the forms, bending, compacting, and rearranging them so that though their conclusive shapes may at first seem arbitrary, they are seen to be pictorial discoveries of the behavior of line, form, and color under the impact of light.

Focal points emphasized here are the head and hands. These suggest light as coming from the upper right. But the subdued effects on the figure suggest lighting from the opposite corner. This is confirmed by the shadow on the right side of the wicker chair. Picasso has visually represented these two opposing directions of light by diagonal lines entering the picture from either upper corner.

Color, which plays upon the forms with unending variety of changing facets, gives credence to the fact that light moves about at will.

PLATE 82

Seated Woman, *Paris, September 23, 1943. Oil on Canvas, 39 x 32".*

In this face the right profile and the left profile interlock and overlap. Furthermore, the composite of both makes the full face.

PLATE 83

Woman in Rocking Chair, *Paris, September 26, 1943. Oil on Canvas, 39 x 28".*

The interlocking profiles here are simpler to identify. The dark profile facing left is convex, and the light profile (with darkened nose), facing right, is concave. The composite of both profiles forms a face in three quarter view.

PLATE 84

Head of a Woman, *Paris, May 27, 1943. Oil on Canvas, 39 x 32″.*

Opposite in treatment to the preceding group in which the curvilinear predominates, the following three portraits of seated women are essentially rectilinear and angular. So strange is the interpretation of these persons that they seem transformed into archaic fetishes, the last one (Plate 87) recalling a New Ireland ceremonial totem.

Discussion is necessarily limited to only a few of the numerous and intricate aspects of Picasso's paintings. The infinite variety of personal invention to be found in specific anatomical features, such as the heads, hands, figures, feet, and their relationship within the picture itself, may be observed throughout his work. For example, the hands in Plate 85, clasped in the woman's lap, are dovetailed (small black hatchings indicate fingers). In Plate 86 one hand is fan-shaped while the other is sawtoothed; and in the next the fingers of one hand are designated as half notes of music, while the construction of the other is like that of a log cabin (Plate 87).

Following this tangent further, the ears at times assume the form of a figure 8, the letter C, a pretzel, an ovoid; the nose is usually a full-grown proboscis of one fantastic shape or another. The eyes, always the fascinating hypnotic focal point in his portraits, show limitless diversity of ideas. Ranging from almost classic verisimilitude to highly idiosyncratic configuration, they include circle, square, crescent, half-moon, triangle, star, trapezoid, lozenge, rhomboid, wedge-shapes, concentric and eccentric ovoids, and many others, all with myriad gradations of change. Their position in relation to each other, as well as to the other features and the head itself, invariably creates new constellations of features.

PLATE 85

Woman Seated in Chair, *Paris, September 1, 1941. Oil on Canvas, 51 x 38".*

PLATE 86

Seated Woman, *Paris, October 23, 1941. Oil on Canvas, 36 x 28".*

PLATE 87

Woman Seated in Chair, *Paris, October 8, 1941. Oil on Canvas, 51 x 38".*

PLATES 88-93

From first to last, this group of portraits is essentially abstract, becoming progressively so as the series proceeds. While all of these are basically human faces, the imagery of mask and skull runs throughout. In the first three portraits the silhouette of the head merges as a skull, upon which eyes and nose appear as a mask. As the group advances, the masked skull is replaced by features closer to human representation. The increasing simplification of the figures results in the surprising fact that while the specific features become more humanized, the over-all paintings become more abstract—another form of the reversal in Picasso's work.

PLATE 88

Seated Woman, *Royan, March 5, 1940. Oil on Canvas, 51 x 38″.*

PLATE 89

Seated Woman, Composition in Gray, *Paris, March 4, 1945. Oil on Canvas, 51 x 38".*

PLATE 90

Portrait of a Woman, *Paris, February 27, 1942. Oil on Wood, 25½ x 21″.*

PLATE 91

Woman with Cigarette Holder, *Paris, August 10, 1942. Oil on Canvas, 25½ x 21″.*

PLATE 92

Portrait of a Woman, *Paris, August 5, 1942. Oil on Canvas, 39 x 32".*

PLATE 93

Seated Nude with Clasped Hands, *Paris, 1941. Oil on Canvas, 36 x 28".*

Essentially two elements working individually and together create equilibrium in this picture. First, there is the action of opposing pulls which comes about in the following way: the main axis is established from upper right to lower left. All along the line of this axis counterthrusts are set up. Further, the forms of the figure build up architectonically. Finally, these forms, in combination with the counterplay of tensions already described, establish an intricate equilibrium. For example: the head upon the apex of the pyramid formed by the neck and shoulders is precariously poised by its own distribution of weight. However, it is held in balance at the top and sides by the framework of surrounding tensions.

PLATE 93

PLATES 94–98

In the grouping that follows, the effect obtained with distortion differs widely from that of the previous groups, for here is an evolution that develops toward surrealist imagery. The portraits, of persons relaxed and tranquil in appearance, are fully modeled, and all except the final one have freely recognizable features. By introducing distortion—an almost taffy-like twisting of the lower jaw—the features simulate a condition of shock akin to religious ecstasy (Plates 96, 97). The unexpected juxtaposition of the literal expression and of distortion endows these portraits with surrealist overtones.

The final picture, although more abstract, gains in surrealist power, for the head seems to be converted into a ritual object of magic.

PLATE 94

Head of a Woman, *Royan, April 2, 1941. Oil on Wood, 18 x 15".*

PLATE 95

The Sailor, *Paris, October 28, 1943. Oil on Canvas, 51 x 32".*

PLATE 96

Seated Woman, *Paris, June 9, 1941. Oil on Canvas, 36 x 23½″.*

PLATE 97

Portrait of a Woman, *Paris, October 18, 1941. Oil on Canvas, 32 x 25½″.*

PLATE 98

Head of a Woman, *Royan, February 3, 1940. Oil on Paper, 25 x 18".*

After a Bacchanale by Poussin, *Paris, August 24, 25, 26, 28, and 29, 1944,*
Gouache, 12 x 16".

Conchita (Daughter of the Artist), *Paris, Aug. 21, 1944. Chinese Ink and Water-Color, 16 x 12″*.

This and the previous plate are reproductions of the two pictures on which Picasso was working during the Battle of the Streets (page 12).

Still Life, Skull of a Bull on a Table, *Paris, April 5, 1942. Oil on Canvas, 51 x 38".*

The motif of death evident in this still life is also suggested by morbid colors: deep browns, purples, greens, and grays. Enacted here is a kind of post-mortem drama. The bull's head, a skull upon a table, is like a death mask set upon the shoulders of one whose cape cloaks his wooden anatomy and whose elbow akimbo suggests a victorious toreador.

PLATE 101

PLATE 102

Skull of a Bull on a Table, *Paris, April 3, 1942. Oil on Canvas, 46 x 35½".*

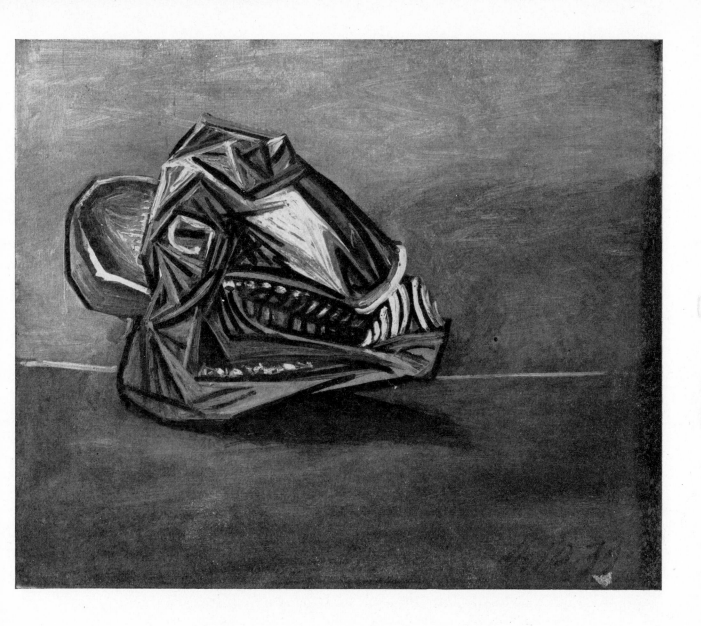

PLATE 103

Head of a Lamb, *Paris, October 4, 1939, Royan. Oil on Canvas, 19¾ x 24″.*

Painted at the beginning of the war and about three years before his *Bull's-head* series.

PLATE 104

Still Life with Chinese Lantern, *Paris, January 15, 1944. Oil on Canvas, 10½ x 18″.*

This picture is a war casualty, the only damage to Picasso's work during the war. The horizontal cut across the Chinese lantern, lower left, was caused by flying glass during a night bombing (Page 4). Color engravings were being made of the picture at the time. The still life depicted, besides the hanging lantern, consists of a crawfish in a dish upon a checkered tablecloth, a moth, and, at the upper right, a starry sky.

PLATE 105

Mother and Child, *Paris, May 21, 1943. Oil on Canvas, 51 x 38".*

Picasso originally painted the child, introducing the mother as an afterthought. His comment on this was: "The child becomes the father of the mother."

PLATE 106

Woman in a Chair, *Paris, November 17, 1941. Oil on Canvas, 28 x 23½".*

PLATE 107

Seated Woman, *Paris, June 14, 1945. Oil on Canvas, 39 x 25½″*.

PLATE 108

Woman Seated, *Paris, April 10, 1944. Oil on Canvas, 17 x 11".*

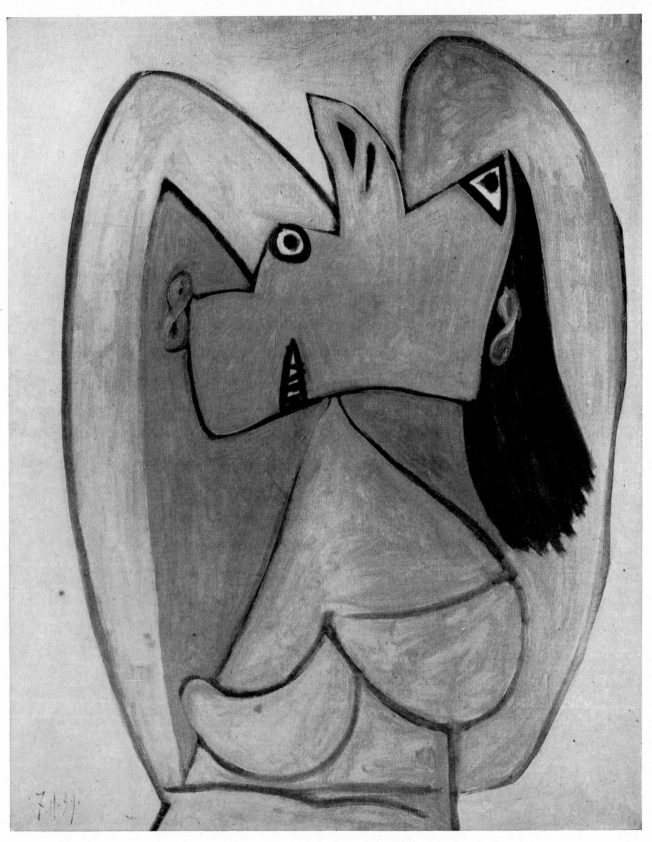

PLATE 109

Half-length Nude, *Royan, November 7, 1939. Oil on Canvas, 32 x 25½"*.

PLATE 110

Woman Seated in a Chair, *Paris, April 12, 1945. Oil on Canvas, 36 x 25½″.*

Coq, Paris, June 17, 1943. Oil on Canvas, 28 x 23½".

PLATE 112

The Kissers, *Paris, December 30, 1943. Oil on Paper, 26 x 20″.*

Study for a detail of *Le Vert-Galant.*

PLATE 113

Paris Scene, Notre Dame at Night, April 18, 1945. Oil on Canvas, 6½ x 10½".

PLATE 114

Paris Scene, *View of Notre Dame, April 14, 1945. Oil on Canvas, 6½ x 10½″.*

A friend, whose lilac garden Picasso had visited, commented upon the unusual coloring in this picture. Picasso replied: "When I returned from your garden, I was so full of lavender, I had to get rid of it."

PLATE 115

Paris Scene, View of Notre Dame, *March 1, 1945. Oil on Canvas, 21 x 32″.*

This is the most abstract variation on this theme.

PLATE 116

Paris Scene, the 14th of July. *Oil on Canvas, 15 x 18".*

On the same day Picasso painted this and a smaller oil, both named for the day—the last pictures he was to paint for many months.

PLATE 117

Still Life with Skull, *Paris, February 27, 1946. Oil on Wood Panel, 32½ x 39½".*

Through association the pitcher seems like a bird of prey, converting the still life into a symbol embodying a vulture and death.

PLATE 118

Still Life with Skull, *Paris, January 3, 1946. Oil on Wood Panel, 22 x 26″*.

The lamp, a traditional symbol of learning, seems like a twenty-first-century personage from another planet. The skull upon the open book paraphrases a skull and bones; again, the teeth bite into the printed page. This picture apparently symbolizes wisdom of the future against the imprint of death upon the pages of history.

PLATE 119

Still Life, *Paris, February 21, 1946. Oil on Wood Panel, 39½ x 32½″.*

This still life and the one reproduced opposite are identical in subject matter. Although the above is an earlier version, it is almost completely abstract. By comparing it with the relatively more representational still life (Plate 120), the objects, a pitcher, a skull, and an open book on a chair, can be more

PLATE 120

Still Life, *Paris, February 26, 1946. Oil on Wood Panel, 52 x 38½″.*

readily identified. Contrasting linear design accounts primarily for the dissimilarity between the two pictures. The still life above, regardless of the surrounding angular structure, has an independent curvilinear identity of its own, while the objects in the other are controlled by the superstructure of rectilinear tensions which forcefully radiate from the core of the composition.

PLATE 121

Figure, *Paris, May 5, 1946. Oil on Canvas, 57½ x 35"*. Unfinished state.

PLATE 122

Figure, *Paris, May 5, 1946. Oil on Canvas, 57½ x 35".*

This is the same canvas in its final state. In the earlier state (left), the head, hair, neck, shoulders, and breasts, Egyptian in feeling, are quite representational. The elongated body, however, already suggests the stem of a plant. Retaining the face, but through slight simplification and shifting of minor details, the figure metamorphoses into a flower.

PLATE 123

Standing Figure of a Woman, *Paris, May 1946. Oil on Canvas, 64 x 38".*

Compare elongated and spherical forms with those in standing figure in Plate 10.

PLATE 124

Seated Woman, *Paris, May 5, 1946. Oil on Canvas, 21½ x 18″*.

A twentieth-century Velasquez.

PLATE 125

Study for Europa, *Paris, June 8, 1946. Oil on Canvas, 51 x 38".*

PLATE 126

The Rape of Europa, *Paris, June 1946. Oil on Canvas, 77 x 51".*

PLATE 127

PLATE 128

Views of Picasso Exhibition of Recent Paintings. *Galerie Louis Carré, Paris, June 1946.*

PLATE 129

Glass Cabinet in Picasso's Studio.

The ancient sculptures and the sculptures and objects by Picasso which fill the case are equally archaic in spirit. On the bottom shelf, center, is an Easter Island hand from which a cast was made and attached to the bronze *La Belle Ferronnière* (Plate 130).

PLATE 130

Bronzes Made During the War.

These and more than a dozen of Picasso's prewar sculptures were cast during the occupation (page 4). The standing woman which Picasso affectionately calls *La Belle Ferronnière* is a curious miscellany: the torso, a silhouette of the 1890s, was cast from a dressmaker's dummy found by Picasso; the hand is a cast of the Easter Island object referred to in Plate 129; Picasso modeled the other members of the figure and welded them into place. Imprints of the corrugated board used in casting provided the high-necked fluted collar.

Below is a horned mask made by welding a pair of handle bars to a bicycle seat. The skull is the first of an edition of two. All the other sculptures in the photograph are unique.

1943   1941
         1942   1941

PLATE 130

1941   February, 1943   1941

PLATE 131

Large Plasters Made During the War.

The subject of *The Shepherd* (center) held Picasso's interest for several months. After doing perhaps one hundred sketches and drawings, he feverishly made the sculpture in a single day.

 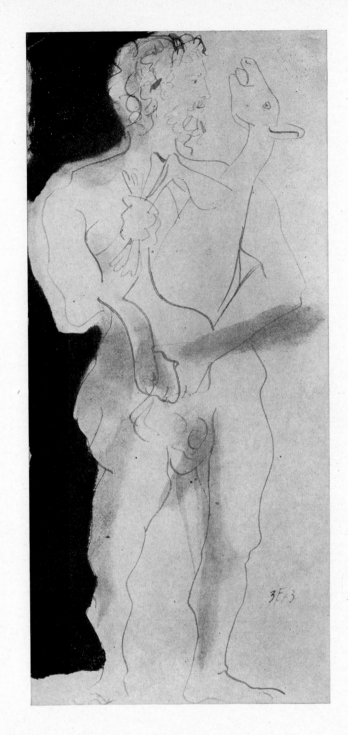

PLATE 132 (left)

Sketch for The Shepherd, *Paris, February 4, 1943. Chinese Ink on Paper, 26 x 8½".*

PLATE 133 (right)

Sketch for The Shepherd, *Paris, February 3, 1943. Chinese Ink on Paper, 24 x 11½".*

PLATE 134

Study for The Shepherd, *Paris, November 29, 1943.*
Oil on Cardboard, 12¾ x 10″.

PLATE 135

Study for The Shepherd, *Paris, November 29, 1943.*
Oil on Cardboard, 12¾ x 10″.

The above studies are painted on the reverse sides
of the same cardboard.

INDEX

INDEX